URBAN BRAZIL

URBAN BRAZIL

Visions, Afflictions, and Governance Lessons

Ivani Vassoler

CAMBRIA
PRESS

YOUNGSTOWN, NEW YORK

Illustration 1 (Brazil map) reproduced with permission from the University of Texas Libraries.
Other illustrations reproduced with permission from the Institute of Research and Urban Planning of Curitiba and Curitiba City Hall.

Library of Congress Cataloging-in-Publication Data

Vassoler, Ivani.
    Urban Brazil : visions, afflictions, and governance lessons / Ivani Vassoler.
        p. cm.
    Includes bibliographical references and index.
    ISBN 978-1-934043-94-3 (alk. paper)
    1. Urban policy—Brazil. 2. City planning—Brazil. 3. Brazil—Social conditions. I. Title.

    HT169.B7V37 2007
    307.760981—dc22

2007037043

To Xuxu, with love

TABLE OF CONTENTS

LIST OF TABLES AND FIGURE

LIST OF ILLUSTRATIONS

FOREWORD

Given my interest in Latin America and urban development in middle-income countries, I was very pleased when Dr. Vassoler requested me to write a foreword for her upcoming book. Prior to my present teaching assignment at Fatih University in Istanbul, Turkey, I had a regular summer teaching assignment at the Universidad de Monterrey in Monterrey, Mexico—a city of approximately 3 million and the third largest in Mexico. Living in Monterrey gave me an up close view of urbanism in Latin America.

I would like to relate one of my experiences, which may illustrate some of the plights of urban living in Latin America. One night, while I was in Monterrey for my teaching stint, I decided to go to the center to have dinner and walk around. While I was in the restaurant eating, a tremendous downpour of rain commenced. I thought by the time I had finished my meal that it would be over, but I had no such luck. I could not walk around in this weather so I went down the street and tried to hail a cab to return home. Every cab driver whom I asked responded that it would not be possible to take me to my neighborhood because the roads were flooded. I was not alone. There were several people at the same corner trying to return home by taxi. Finally, I was able to convince a taxi driver to take me to my apartment by offering him 100 pesos—almost triple the normal rate to my home. Believe me, this was a very uncomfortable ride as I did not know exactly if we could make it there. Fortunately, my particular area was not flooded and I was able to get home safely.

I was fortunate because the next day in the news, there were reports of drownings, stranded cars, and flooded neighborhoods. New plans were proposed to have better drainage and citizen representatives-advocates urged the municipal government to do something. The annual flooding in June (the time when I taught) was not new but had been agravated by unrestricted urbanization, which created more impervious surfaces and eliminated the sparse vegetation that would normally have decreased the runoff. The municipal governments also were unable to prevent homes to be constructed in flood plains, so there was either houses lost or people drowned when these flash floods occurred. This is just one example of the problems that urban residents in Latin America experience, but demonstrates the lack of planning and inadequate municipal management that is found in other Latin American cities.

Cities in Latin America would appear to have a host of insurmountable problems, such as severe pollution, chronic traffic congestion, rapidly growing populations, strained infrastructues, illegal housing, corruption, and an unequal distribution of wealth. There are numerous books and articles lamenting these circumstances in Latin America. However, instead of feeding the reader the same "warmed-over" material, Dr. Vassoler presents a success story of the experience in Curitiba, and ultimately a message of hope to other Latin American cities. The underlying message of her book is that progress can be made in confronting the problems of urbanization in Latin America, and the "Curitiba experience" can be used as a "blueprint" for other efforts of urban managment in this region.

By detailing the journey of municipal governments of Curitiba, Brazil, and the success in solving many of its urban problems, while cities such as São Paulo languish, the present work gives us the complete background of how this situation came about. What is amazing is that the public in Curitiba not only is engaged in the planning process, but elects public officials based on their commitment to it. Also, the solutions proposed and projects were not grandiose and unrealistic, but innovative and within the resources of the city. Curitiba is now recognized in urban planning literature as a model city, particularly in terms of solving traffic congestion by the means of an extensive network of exclusive bus lanes or Bus Rapid Transit—which is much less expensive than fixed rail. In addition, this comprehensive bus network can handle just as many passengers as a light rail system. The hallmark of the "Curitiba experiment" is to execute low-cost projects in a reasonable time period. Dr. Vassoler gives the full background of these remarkable developments and the details of the decision-making process behind them.

This book should be a must for anyone interested in Latin American urbanization and urban planning/administration. If you are a professor who teaches Latin America or urban planning, this book should be placed on your reading list for your students. It should become a guidebook for those involved in the governing of Latin American cities and other cities in middle-income economies, which share many similar problems. I would hope that citizen advocates in Latin America urban areas would pick up this book, show it to their local politicians, and point out that there is no need to wait for someday in the future for things to get better. Those involved in urban planning and city administration in high-income countries should also find much to garner from this book.

Hopefully, we will see many more books from Dr. Vassoler as this one was intelligent, insightful, and a pleasure to read.

Michael A. McAdams
Geography Department
Fatih University
Istanbul, Turkey

PREFACE

Although governance problems in Brazil at the federal, state, and local levels are well known, less attention has been given to cases in which the government works well. Without denying, hiding, or minimizing the serious policy flaws and the unfortunate existence of dishonest politicians and public officials tampering with public funds in a country characterized by a great deal of social injustice, this book takes a different course by striking a more positive tone regarding what governments can do to promote the common good. Having as a backdrop the sweeping transformations that took place in Brazil in the last quarter of the 20th century as a result of intense urbanization, modernization, and industrialization, this work assesses the challenges and opportunities city governments face in addressing the numerous shortcomings of urban life in the largest Latin American country.

Rather than focusing on the best places to live, I started this research with the aim of examining the dynamics of city governments, how they operate and in the end how their actions do or do not contribute to making city life more bearable. Curitiba, the capital of the Paraná State, is unlike much of the rest of Brazil in terms of the positive outcomes that have resulted from local government intervention in the process of urban reform. Although there is no such thing as a perfect urban reform process, the situation in Curitiba is worth examining because of the beneficial impact urban reform has had on the lives of the city residents in the form of improvements to and the expansion of the provision of public services. The urban development process in Curitiba offers a unique opportunity to study government and politics: it is a case that combines city leadership with an innovative plan to transform a chaotic provincial town into a more livable metropolis. In the early 1960s, this type of urban vision marked a total departure from the conventional way in which local governments in other Brazilian cities were dealing with the challenges posed by urban growth. The fact that almost 40 years later, the same planning instrument, enacted by legislation in 1965, continues to orient the urban development process in Curitiba—and that other city governments, both in Brazil and elsewhere, are looking for guidance from the Curitiba case—indicates that the urban vision of its past may offer lessons to the present.

The decision-making process behind the urban reforms in Curitiba is this book's main theme. After extended periods of fieldwork in that city and in São Paulo, Brazil's largest metropolis, I was able to identify some of the government attributes that foster more harmonious policy environments, which in turn lead to more coherent public policies. Through my interviews with urban planners, politicians, scholars, and residents, and after the analysis of hundreds of policy documents, pieces of legislation, press reports and scholarly studies, I developed an analytical model that draws on the insights of urban regime theory in which one of the most important tenets is the role of public entrepreneurs as agents of change within the municipal sphere.

By focusing on the dynamics of successive local governments in Curitiba for almost 40 years and examining the urban planning decision-making process and assessing the public policy outcomes and their impact on public service delivery, I hope to convey the notion that the municipal sphere can be redefined for the better. In this sense, this book should be seen as an attempt to rescue the impaired image of governments, in an age when there is a temptation to privatize public services in the name of market efficiency. There is no reason here to go to great lengths on the basics of political economy; we just have to return to Adam Smith to remember that market efficiency is dependent on government efficacy.

ACKNOWLEDGMENTS

In memory of Milton Santos (1926–2001), Brazilian urban geographer and social critic, for his seminal work on urbanization and his struggles for a more equitable urban development process worldwide.

The research behind this book was made possible, thanks to the support of several people. I am grateful to the late Professor Milton Santos, who, despite his poor health, gracefully received me for an interview in his office at the University of São Paulo. I am equally thankful to Jorge Wilheim, Cândido Malta Campos Filho, and Jaime Lerner, all accomplished Brazilian urban planners and scholars of urbanization, who took the time to share their knowledge with me.

I am forever indebted to Professor Maria José Menezes Lourega Belli from the Federal University in Curitiba for all the assistance, company, and support she provided me from the very first day I arrived in Curitiba several years ago. I also thank Maria José for introducing me to her university colleague, Professor Dennison de Oliveira, who shared his views on urban planning and referred me to another accomplished scholar, Professor Nelson Rosário de Souza. My gratitude goes also to Dr. Ana Evans de Carvalho, from the Universidade Nova Lisboa, Portugal, for her warm-hearted friendship and empathy, and for her valuable intellectual insights, which have enhanced the theoretical and methodological scope of my research project.

This work also benefited enormously from Brazilian scholars and professionals working with the Institute of Research and Urban Planning of Curitiba (IPPUC), the Paraná Institute of Socioeconomic Development (IPARDES) and the São Paulo-based Center for Policy Studies in Municipal Administration (CEPAM). The anonymous employees of those institutions and the staff members at the Curitiba Public Library and the Central Library of the Federal University of Paraná facilitated my access to archives and to a variety of publications, and I thank them for that support. I also acknowledge here the assistance provided by Jorge Samek; by João Pedro Amorin, former Curitiba City Hall Press Secretary, and Ms. Duda Camargo, former assistant to the Governor of the State of Paraná, during my stays in Curitiba.

A warm thanks to Nesta de Vizia and Lea Menezes Lourega—Curitiba residents—whose affection and hospitality I will never forget.

Scattered throughout the Americas are my dear friends who, in different times and in distinct ways, have provided all kinds of support including encouragement, exchange of ideas, sources of information, and insights on urban life in the places that they live in Brazil, Mexico, Uruguay, and the United States. My sincere thanks to all of them, with a special recognition to Marina D'Andrea, a courageous woman, a respected journalist, one of the forces behind the development of the Brazilian feminist press, and above all a dear friend who did not live to read the book that she knew I would complete. Wherever she is, I know she is rooting for me.

Likewise, I am grateful to Professors Karol Soltan, Ken Conca, and William Hanna, from the University of Maryland, for their support and timely academic advice. My thanks as well to Michael McAdams, a committed scholar and urban planner for his comments on this work, and for the opportunity to learn from him the dynamics of urbanization in other parts of the world; to Robert Loper and Joanne Foeller for their sound editorial assistance; to the hardworking Cambria Press professionals for their unwavering support; and to Grenda Vassoler, who contributed with archival research during my fieldwork in São Paulo.

I also express an enormous gratitude to my extended family in São Paulo for their endless support and affection. Finally, I am eternally grateful to my husband who has always believed in me more than I have; he is and has been my everlasting source of encouragement, motivation, and optimism. This book would not be possible without him (and this is absolutely serious). He has my eternal love.

Earlier versions of portions of this manuscript were presented at academic conferences. The institutions and persons mentioned above are not responsible for and do not necessarily agree with the analysis and points of view presented in this book, which are my entire responsibility.

ACRONYMS

ACP	*Associação Comercial do Paraná*
	Paraná Chamber of Commerce
ARENA	*Aliança Renovadora Nacional*
	Alliance for National Renewal
CEMPRE	*Compromisso Empresarial Para Reciclagem*
	Entrepreneurial Commitment for Recycling
CIC	*Cidade Industrial de Curitiba*
	Curitiba Industrial City
CNDU	*Conselho Nacional de Desenvolvimento Urbano*
	National Council for Urban Development
COHAB	*Companhia Municipal de Habitação*
	Municipal Housing Company
CURA	*Comunidades Urbanas de Recuperação Acelerada*
	Urban Communities of Accelerated Recuperation

EBTU   *Empresa Brasileira de Transportes Urbanos*
                Brazilian Urban Transportation Agency
FMH   *Fundo Municipal de Habitação*
                Municipal Housing Fund
IBAM   *Instituto Brasileiro de Administração Municipal*
                Brazilian Institute for Municipal Administration
IBGE   *Instituto Brasileiro de Geografia e Estatística*
                Brazilian Institute of Geography and Statistics
IPARDES   *Instituto Paranaense de Desenvolvimento*
                Econômico e Social
                Paraná Institute for Socioeconomic Development
IPPUC   *Instituto de Pesquisa e Planejamento Urbano*
                de Curitiba
                Institute of Research and Urban Planning of
                Curitiba
MDB   *Movimento Democrático Brasileiro*
                Brazilian Democratic Movement
PDT   *Partido Democrático Trabalhista*
                Democratic Labor Party
PMD   *Partido do Movimento Democrático Brasileiro*
                Brazilian Democratic Movement Party
PT   *Partido dos Trabalhadores*
                Workers' Party
UNILIVRE   *Universidade Livre do Meio Ambiente*
                Open Environmental University
URBS   *Urbanização Curitiba*
                Curitiba Urbanization Regulatory Agency

INTRODUCTION

Divine Nature gave the fields, human art built the cities.
—Marcus Terentius Varro (116 BC–27 BC),
Roman naval officer and man of letters who wrote
hundreds of scholarly pieces of which only two books
survive: *De Lingua Latina* and *De Re Rustica.*

Amid the harsh realities of daily life that confront city residents in Latin America, there are some reasons for optimism concerning the level and quality of essential public services citizens can expect from local government. Although rapid globalization constrains governmental action in Latin America, there is evidence that local governments within the continent can make a positive difference in the lives of city residents. Latin America has high levels of urbanization, and the region's cities struggle with an array of problems, including air pollution, crime, traffic jams, inadequate public transportation, and precarious housing. It is therefore important to assess the capabilities of local governments and understand how they can address these challenges and improve living conditions of urban residents.

The research presented here focuses on the capabilities of local governments with the unit of analysis being the urban development process in Curitiba, the capital of the state of Paraná, in the south of Brazil. For more than 35 years, this process has guided the impressive growth and transformation of Curitiba, which stands out as an example of effective governance in a country where there is widespread pessimism about government performance at all levels—federal, state, and local. Far from exemplifying such over-publicized slogans as a "model city," "first world city," or "green city," Curitiba and its urban development process offer lessons in local governance that are in striking contrast to the record of public service delivery evident in other Latin American cities.

In Brazil, the inability of city governments to deliver public services is, in addition to being a major national concern, the daily bread and butter topic of political commentators. Official data indicate that 77% of the country's city halls are involved in grave irregularities, which include mismanagement, misappropriation of funds, and the use of public office for personal benefit. The low regard local public officials have for the quality of urban life is further illustrated by the fact that only 30% of the 5,000 Brazilian municipalities have implemented an urban planning process, even though a 1991 federal law makes this type of action mandatory.

Yet if these conditions mark Brazil's present, there are ongoing changes that suggest that the future of local governance could be very different. The process of democratization and its by-products—fiscal and political decentralization— have led local governments in Latin America, and particularly in Brazil, to increase their profile in national politics. The popular legitimacy conferred by free elections, the support of constituencies, and the financial resources at their disposal (either raised by local taxes or coming from federal transfers) put city governments in the position of being agents of change. By virtue of their responsibility for public services such as transportation, garbage collection, and urban renewal, local governments have the potential to make city living less hard than it is. The perennial difficulty is in making this happen. This book suggests that the municipal sphere itself can be redefined to mitigate better urban afflictions.

My search for explanations of productive municipal public policies in mass transportation and environmental quality has led me to examine the local decision-making process in the city of Curitiba over a period of 35 years. The inquiry produced a central theme: a combination of political commitment, consensus-building capabilities, and knowledgeable city organizations contribute to a more harmonious policy environment, which in turn offers incentives for better governance practices. In practical terms, a coherent governance strategy can be discerned in the transformation of Curitiba from a lackluster and disorganized city to a dynamic urban center that serves today as a reference for urban planners both in Brazil and abroad. The positive

impact of this governance strategy can be seen in the provision of public services, as Curitiba is recognized for its
state-of-the-art public transportation system and for several
sensible and incremental municipal programs to promote
environmental education, to create and preserve green
areas, and reverse urban decay.

Students of politics will find the urban development
process in Curitiba to be an interesting case, as they will
observe that several governing groups, affiliated with different political parties, have adhered to the same governance
strategy. As a result, urban policies have had time to mature
and produce successful outcomes. This type of harmonious
policy environment has had a doubly contagious effect. On
the one hand, local politics has become more reliable, as the
guiding principle of city politics is the enhancement of the
urban development process. On the other, the government
focus on urban planning has generated a completely new
city mentality in which residents, from all walks of life, feel
comfortable enough to talk about the urban programs in
place, how they evolved, and how they could be improved.
This is a type of urban culture that is seldom seen in other
parts of Brazil. Because they know what their governments
can accomplish, Curitiba residents are in a position to
demand more of local politicians.

There is a persistent claim that Curitiba is so unique that its
public policies cannot be replicated in other Brazilian or Latin
American cities. Yet this objection is misleading because the
point is not to transfer simply successful policies from one
setting to another. Urban spaces are not created equal, and
policies that worked in a particular environment may not

work in others. By contrasting the governance strategies in Curitiba with those in São Paulo, Brazil's largest city, I see that the single most important governance lesson that the Curitiba case offers is not what has been accomplished there but how it was done. The innovative urban experiment that emerged in Curitiba is above all an invitation to reflect on how governments can govern better.

Any work focusing on positive experiences in government runs the risk of being considered as propaganda. But what follows here is a critical assessment of an urban development process, which is not without imperfections and which is not an unmitigated success. Almost 40 years later, urban reform in the capital of Paraná is facing challenges, especially as a result of growth in the metropolitan area. In my view, the merits of examining what has happened in Curitiba go beyond the importance of the improvements in essential public services. The real focus is on the capabilities of local governments to accomplish what they are supposed to do: govern. Ultimately, the Curitiba experience in urban development may also hold lessons for local governments in Africa and Asia, which are at an earlier state in the process of urbanization. The urban experiment in Curitiba suggests that, given the right policy response, the worst consequences of fast urban growth can be tamed.

This book is organized into five chapters. Chapter 1 situates the urban development process in Curitiba in the larger context of urbanization in Brazil. The analysis focuses on the urban transformations in 20th century Brazil, and the changes that have occurred in local politics as a result of the process of democratization that started in the 1980s.

The chapter also contrasts the divergent paths taken by local governments both in Curitiba and São Paulo regarding urban growth and public policy.

Chapter 2 examines the urban reforms in Curitiba, having as a starting point the enactment in 1965 of a sensible urban policy instrument, officially called the *Plano Diretor* (Master Plan). This plan soon became the ultimate tool for successive governments to deal with city growth and the challenges posed by intense urbanization. The chapter proceeds with a systematic analysis of what municipal authorities have accomplished with the implementation of the Master Plan, particularly examining the public transportation and environmental management policies.

The comprehensive urban development process in Curitiba, based on an urban vision that calls for an integrative approach to deal with the city's woes, did not emerge by chance. To explain this complex process of urban reform, chapter 3 presents my analytical model for institutional change and its applicability to the politics of urban development in Curitiba. Chapter 4 contains an explanatory discussion of the succession of policy failures in the city of São Paulo with an analysis of the municipal decision-making process of different city administrations. The final chapter offers a synthesis of the main arguments and explores the lessons that the urban experiment in Curitiba may offer to those concerned with the quality of life in cities around the world.

URBAN BRAZIL

CHAPTER 1

STUDYING URBAN GOVERNANCE

Gentlemen, there isn't a body without cells. The state does
not exist without municipalities. Living matter does not exist
without organic life. Thus, we cannot conceive a nation without a state, without municipal life.

—Ruy Barbosa[1]

This book recounts the origins, evolution, and outcomes of one
of the most singular urban development experiments ever put
in place in the developing world. The planning process in the
city of Curitiba, Brazil, was so innovative (and to some extent
still is) that scholars and policymakers to this day do not agree
on its significance. Urban environments in less-developed

countries are marked by great inequalities, and urban development programs are often evaluated by how they deal with this issue. Academics from different schools of thought, and often with different political agendas, have assessed the Curitiba experiment and delivered everything from rosy assessments to staunch rebukes. Others have focused on the idea of replicability or policy diffusion, and have sought to identify ways by which the successes of the Curitiba experiment can be applied elsewhere. Whereas this latter concern has great promise, it can also be misleading. Cities are different organisms whose sometimes similar pathologies require distinct remedies. Curitiba does not offer a "one-size-fits-all" solution to the problems of urban development.

Yet there are surely lessons to be learnt from different urban development processes. Barbara Czarniawska, in her study of three European capitals, compared cities to laboratories in being the birthplaces of invention, innovation, and imitation.[2] At the dawn of the 21st century, Curitiba, the capital of the Paraná state, located in the south of Brazil, is arguably one of very few cities in the developing world that stands as a positive reference for urban planning. The urban experiment in Curitiba has been guided in part by the goal of mitigating hardships caused by urbanization. This focus has helped to advance the notion of citizenship rights—that all city residents, rich and poor, should have access to the public spaces and services provided by the municipality. In this sense, the urban planning model that has accompanied Curitiba's growth for the last 40 years can be seen as a response to the preoccupations of Henri Lefebvre in his seminal work on "the right to the city."[3]

Lefebvre's central thesis offers a radical view of urban politics that argues for city control to be transferred from the national and state levels to urban inhabitants. Curitiba's urban development process reflects a more modern and updated version of this belief: the implementation of public policies should promote the notion that all urban dwellers have a right to enjoy public spaces and access city services.[4] In tangible terms, the results of the strategy in Curitiba can be seen in a state-of-the-art public transportation system and an innovative environmental management strategy based on a system of multiple urban parks, an incremental program of waste recycling, and an array of environmental education initiatives at the school and community levels. Simple as these public policies may be, they are truly pioneering in Brazil, where city governments find it difficult to establish programs to deal with these essential elements of the urban space.

My field research has led me to think in different ways about the lessons that the city of Curitiba may offer to policymakers and others concerned with the quality of urban life around the world. Rather than ask whether specific urban programs adopted in Curitiba are or would be feasible in other cities, my goal is to assess Curitiba's policy environment to understand how the innovations in urban development emerged and why they flourished there. The lessons, therefore, should not be taken as a recipe for the emulation of policies but rather be seen as examples of how governments can act and what they can accomplish. In this sense, the examination of the urban experiment in Curitiba is one way to answer a perennial question in political science, one that was articulated more than a decade ago: How do we best govern?[5]

This question has a pressing prominence in Brazil, where an atmosphere of widespread pessimism prevails regarding the quality of governance at both the federal and local levels. To a large extent, democratization in Brazil has not increased government efficacy. Political pluralism, free elections, and the benefits of a free press have not led elected and nonelected public officials to govern better, and a devoted commitment to the public good is still rare in Brazil. Thus far, the empowerment of local governments—the by-product of democratization that raised hopes for improved provision of public services in urban Brazil—is far from meeting its expectations.

During my field research, this disregard for the public good was nowhere more conspicuous than in São Paulo, Brazil's largest city, and similar to Curitiba, a state capital. While working in São Paulo in the early 2000s, I observed a Latin American metropolis in shambles, facing an unprecedented political and administrative chaos that was the culmination of decades of mismanagement and damaging policies. Garbage collections were routinely suspended, municipal health services had collapsed, the city's few green areas had been transformed into trash fields, and the public transportation system was in complete disarray. The situation was so depressing that radio talk show commentators were thanking God for the imminent departure of Mayor Celso Pitta, who concluded his term in disgrace amid charges of influence peddling and the use of public office for personal benefits. One wag described São Paulo as the "Pitanic," comparing the city to the famous sinking ship. Pitta's legacy was to leave the city with an astonishing debt of US$9 billion without relevant public work projects to show for it. His most promising project—an elevated bus corridor—remained for years an amorphous piece of concrete, supported by rusty iron rods. It was, in effect, a white elephant crossing a central area of the city linking nowhere to nothing.

How could the country's wealthiest city, with a fine educated middle class and world-class urban planners, fall so low? To those who live, work, and study in São Paulo, the deterioration in and neglect of basic city services are not related to the size of the city or an alleged lack of financial resources. During my interviews, there was never a single word to suggest that São Paulo is simply ungovernable because of the size of its population. Many observers have expressed amazement at its gradual urban decay, which should be unthinkable in a metropolis that accounts for a significant chunk of Brazil's gross domestic product (GDP). There is a kind of mantra in São Paulo, suggesting that the city can be governed better. This has led *Paulistanos* and many Brazilians to believe that the city's problems are the result of an inexplicable sequence of dismal local governments. In the absence of a more convincing explanation, folk talk has attributed the situation to an improbable bout of bad luck.

Of course luck, either good or bad, cannot explain the contrasts in governance strategies between São Paulo and Curitiba. Jaime Lerner, one of Brazil's most popular mayors (he was Curitiba's mayor for three terms) used to say "tendency is not destiny." His mantra was that if Curitiba has changed, others could as well. How then can we explain variations in governance in large and relatively prosperous urban centers subject to identical constraints imposed by national politics and the national political economy? Over the period from 1965 to 2000—the timeline of this analysis—successive city governments in São Paulo and Curitiba faced daunting challenges posed by increasing socioeconomic inequalities, the country's inequitable model of development, and the absence of a coherent national urban policy amid a chaotic and intense process of urbanization. Although constrained by these factors, the Curitiba and São Paulo governments also had abundant resources at their disposal, due to their centrality as state capitals in the south-southeast corridor, Brazil's most developed region. My analysis of 35 years of the decision-making process and public policy environment in Curitiba, in comparison with public policies in São Paulo during the same time period, emphasizes the explanatory power of the path dependence model[6] and the positive influence of government attributes such as political commitment, consensus building, and organizational capabilities. Path-dependent evolution of government policies and programs can lock in particular approaches and make it difficult to change course. Within this environment, positive government attributes can make it easier for local officials, acting as public entrepreneurs, to establish productive policy frameworks for designing, implementing, and improving city programs.

The message I hope to convey in this work is that despite the atmosphere of pessimism in Brazil, born from years of experience with unresponsive governments, there are opportunities for making urban life much better—if governments are committed to doing so. Yet frustration may grow if those concerned with the quality of urban life limit themselves to the mere replication of public policies that are working in a different setting. Urban areas within the same country present enormous variation in demands and available resources. Therefore, those who hope to improve urban life should go beyond the simple emulation of policies and instead work to build a policy environment that encourages more productive public actions.

What follows is not, by any means, a cultural narrative of cities or a description of a model city. It is neither a comparison of bad and good urban spaces nor a tale of utopian views of futurist metropolises. Moreover, although the research discusses urban planning, I do not deal with technical aspects of the subject but focus instead on the politics of planning. The main themes of this book are governance strategies and their impact on the quality of government action at the municipal level. The chapters that follow provide a critical examination of the public policy environment during more than three decades of decision-making in the city of Curitiba and contrast its governance strategy with that of São Paulo's. The examination of two urban programs—mass transportation and environmental management (and a subset of initiatives derived from them)—provides the content on which the policy frameworks are assessed. The analysis reveals how local politics shapes and is shaped by either a coherent or a confusing policy environment in urban spaces marked by inequalities. Throughout the work as a whole, the perennial question—how do we best govern?—is a central theme.

THE INQUIRY AND EXPLANATORY FACTORS

The concept of governance examined in this book goes beyond the notion of government understood merely as a group in power. As governance is a process, the analysis of problems and opportunities in a given political unit should not be limited to the examination of a single government but rather cover a sequence of governments and their actions for a determined period of time. The United Nations Center for Human Settlements defines good urban governance as a process "by which the common good is increased, with the common good being all things which make up a decent quality of life and good society."[7]

Although good governance is not the cure for all urban ills, it increases the likelihood of better city living. Assessments of governmental action conducted by the United Nations and the UK-based Building and Social Housing Foundation show that depending on governmental actions or inactions, governance can be either effective or incompetent, can improve over time, or take a turn for the worse. Whereas governance strategies will differ in response to specific conditions of urban spaces, the ultimate goal of a good governance practice is steady improvement in the common good.

Once implemented, urban programs offer subsequent administrations incentives to keep—or even enhance—them. It is plausible to assume that governance will be better or more effective when a given governing group perceives the possibility of better outcomes and commits itself to and embarks on what it sees as a more satisfactory set of policies. Conversely, when the likelihood of better outcomes is not perceived, a commitment to implementing urban improvements is less likely, which also reduces the likelihood of more satisfactory policies. Under these circumstances, governments remain prisoners of damaging policies, leading to a poorer governance strategy.

The logical questions to ask then are how or under what conditions this ability to implement more satisfactory policies emerges, and how the course of damaging policies can be altered. The literature on urban politics in the United States reveals a great number of local government initiatives that have transformed urban spaces through the modernization of municipal public services, elimination of bureaucratic inefficiencies, and creation of economic enhancements.[8] My search for factors that can influence the quality of government performance found a cogent explanation in the path dependence model. One of the most important assumptions of that analytical framework is that because policy environments are self-reinforcing, governments can be captives of unsatisfactory public programs and find it hard, if not impossible, to change direction.[9] As Anthony Woodlief argued in 1998, path dependency can explain why some urban governments get "locked into" poor policies. Once a local government implements a garbage collection program or invests in an urban renewal project, the self-reinforcing nature of the policy environment makes it easier to continue the program or project than to revise or terminate it.

Resistance to policy change can come from many sources. It can be the result of interest groups acting on their own behalf, bureaucrats who have incentives to preserve and expand programs under their administration, or even entire municipal bureaucracies operating according to their own rules independent of city hall. The multiple sources of resistance to change have led some scholars to focus on the characteristics of those local governments that are more successful than others in changing policy direction. Douglas Yates, for instance, has argued that satisfactory responses to urban problems are intrinsically related to the ability of local public officials to shape the policy arena. Local officials who are able to escape the cycle of damaging policies have been labeled "public entrepreneurs," following Joseph Schumpeter's work on innovation and entrepreneurial behavior.[10] Mark Schneider and Paul Tesk, for instance, have equated public entrepreneurs to agents of change who "...inject innovation into the practices of their own local governments, which can then diffuse throughout the entire system of government...while public entrepreneurs seek to maximize their own profits, they produce benefits that others garner. And just like economic entrepreneurs, public entrepreneurs provide important pecuniary externalities to the other actors in the system."[11] In a similar vein, Don Lavoie observed in 1991 that public entrepreneurs examine a given situation in a manner that is qualitatively different from that of others; this ability, he speculates, seems to be a consequence of a higher degree of sensitivity toward the needs of others.

By focusing this analysis on the concept of public entrepreneurship, I am leaving aside other powerful explanations for government performance. In 1993, Robert Putnam, for instance, developed the notion of social capital to answer the critical question of why some governments are more successful than others. His important study about the performance of regional governments in Italy concluded that a greater degree of civic involvement, measured by levels of community association, interpersonal trust, and cooperation, accounts for better governance strategies. Another compelling explanation of government success—economic development—received support from Robert Fried and Francine Rabinovitz, who concluded that "of all of the theories to explain the performance difference, the most powerful one is modernization."[12] Although I do not question these explanations, my focus on government attributes is the result of my thinking that despite the importance of civil society organizations, governments do matter. In fact, it is possible to think in terms of the reverse relationship: improvements in governance can lead to higher levels of civic engagement. To some extent, as I observed in Curitiba, better governance strategies have the power to mobilize society. Government action toward improvements in the delivery of public services and public campaigns to promote citizens' rights created a new mentality focusing on urban enhancements and led residents to demand better governments.

Although social capital, in the form of interpersonal trust and local associations, may improve the quality of government programs, this outcome is not necessarily always the case. The literature on development studies, citing World Bank data, indicates that local organizations, in a given society, often do not share the same goals. Different groups try to influence government policy to their own advantage and to the detriment of others. Also, if high levels of social capital are linked to good governance, how can we account for instances of good government practices in countries where levels of social capital are low?

In 1997, two books focusing on disparate cases provided, however, comparable answers to this question. In one case, Kathryn Stoner-Weiss confronted the issue in her study of governments in Russia. She found cases of responsive governments in several Russian provinces, despite the nonexistence, according to her, of strong civic communities. In these cases, Stoner-Weiss determined that leadership was a much more cogent explanation for government performance. In another case, Judith Tendler reported similar findings in her analysis of good government performance in Ceará, one of the states located in the northeast of Brazil, the country's most impoverished region. Ceará is plagued by a chronic inland drought, with the result that the state capital, Fortaleza, is swollen with peasants escaping starvation and lack of economic opportunities. Yet despite poverty, clientelistic politics, and low levels of civic engagement in the area, Tendler's study details how a new governor with a reformist agenda revamped the state public sector and developed efficient state and municipal programs to enhance agricultural productivity and to improve preventive health care.

There are very few studies focusing on social capital in Brazil, but the results indicate that existing levels are low. In one of these studies, Marcelo Costa Ferreira has identified the existence of both "a predatory civic culture" and an "associational alienation," in Brazil, suggesting that the participation of individuals in community groups and neighborhood associations occurs mainly as a means for obtaining personal benefits. The same can be said about labor unions' affiliation.[13] Therefore, and following Putnam's reasoning, the dismal level of social capital in Brazil may well help us to understand why the country faces governance problems. However how, in this context, can we explain better governance strategies?

Rather than disregarding other explanations, my focus on public entrepreneurs is intended to increase the analytical scope for understanding public policy formation and governance strategies in cities in the developing world. In analyzing the process of introducing innovation into the public sector, the public entrepreneurship model can be used to evaluate governments and their ability to act under a variety of circumstances, including budgetary constraints and the demands posed by intense urbanization.[14]

Finally, a few words about city size must be mentioned, keeping in mind that governing large urban spaces is not a trivial task. The degree to which the quality of governance strategies and government performance is determined by the size of population is a question that remains open. In fact, by singling out size as the sole factor influencing the quality of government action, we run the risk of minimizing the extent of positive outcomes in large cities and serious governance problems in smaller ones. As Edward Glaeser stressed in 1999, "cities are not bad because of size, but rather because they are ill governed."[15]

URBANIZATION: PAST AND PRESENT

The contrasts between the governance strategies that guided the urban experiment in Curitiba and those that informed the less successful approaches seen elsewhere in Brazil must be understood within the context of the intense process of urbanization that engulfed the country in the 1960s. A rural exodus of huge proportions took place as millions of impoverished countryside dwellers were forced to leave their homes due to modernization, industrialization, and the mechanization of the agricultural sector. According to some estimates, in a 10-year period beginning in the 1960s, about 13 million people left the rural areas to live in the cities; in the next decade, the number increased to 15 million. In search of economic opportunities, peasants found their way to the state capitals of the south-southeast corridor, particularly São Paulo, Rio de Janeiro, Belo Horizonte, Curitiba, and Porto Alegre.

That massive transfer of people from rural to urban areas coincided with the cycle of authoritarian politics that started in Brazil with the 1964 military coup. State capitals became critical units in the military's strategy to promote the country's modernization and industrialization through public and foreign investments. Yet that development model, characterized by great inequality in income distribution, generated a series of distortions that accentuated the negative effects of urbanization in the form of swollen cities and a lack of public services. With the state capitals becoming loci of social unrest due to poverty and street violence, the military regime decided to exercise territorial control of the major urban centers by designating them as "national security areas." As part of this strategy, they suspended popular elections for mayors in state capitals; instead the appointment was made by governors, who in turn were nominated by the military rulers.

Although the military's rule (1964–1985) entailed a great degree of centralization, political repression, and violation of human rights, local governments did enjoy some level of autonomy due to their ability to collect municipal taxes. This gave them limited freedom to design and implement public policies.[16] However, against a backdrop of strong political authoritarianism, moderate-to-high administrative centralization, profound changes in the economic structure of society, and unsettling population shifts, city governments around the country faced significant challenges and constraints. They were unprepared to deal with the arrival of huge contingents of new residents as the country as a whole lacked a comprehensive national urban development strategy. Dislocations produced by the national economic model exacerbated existing urban problems, most critically in the areas of public transportation and adequate housing. The housing crisis triggered a perverse process of land occupation and illegal human settlements, which led to a number of deleterious consequences, including contamination of water resources and degradation of the urban environment.

The governance strategy that evolved in Curitiba, following implementation of the city master plan (*Plano Diretor*) in 1965, was founded on a common agreement that the city needed a consistent and comprehensive but flexible blueprint for its future. One of the plan's distinctive features was its large scope in focusing on both the physical and social aspects of urban development. This breadth of detail made it easier for successive governments to control city policy-making and develop more effective policies for dealing with the changing urban space. The positive results achieved in Curitiba are encouraging, compared to the outcomes produced in other Brazilian cities; they highlight the importance of governments' internal dynamics for understanding the distinct responses to the urban challenges that emerged in the 1960s.

The pervasive presence of Curitiba's master plan in virtually all aspects of city affairs has led to a self-reinforcing urban development process. New generations of politicians and policymakers have learned to take it into account as part of the policymaking environment to such a degree that no serious electoral aspirant can afford to ignore it. This stands in contrast to other city governments in Brazil, where urban development is dealt with in a more improvised fashion and new claimants to power often ignore or derail existing plans. In the four decades covered by this book, for instance, different São Paulo governments developed several master plans, all of which essentially remained in the drawer.[17] None of them adequately addressed pressing city maladies, either because the policy proposals were vague or misguided or because divergences among city hall, city agencies, and legislators prevented effective government action. Whereas it is clear that Brazil's largest city has the human capital and financial means to address urban problems, the city has long been victim of ill-conceived policies. Jorge Wilheim, a renowned urban planner with deep knowledge of São Paulo, attributes its urban decay to the "suicidal sclerosis" of successive municipal administrations. In 1965, Wilheim had asserted that, "in a moment when everybody is calling attention to the importance of the city for the civilization's future, and to the necessity of adapting cities to the lives of millions of citizens, we witness in São Paulo the sleepy practice of laissez-faire that already granted to our city the title of one in the world where life is the worst."

Yet São Paulo, which has been described by urban experts as "a laboratory of urban planning missteps,"[18] was until the early 1960s a city that had fascinated foreigners by its diversity, growth, energy, and wealth. It embodied Brazilian dreams of modernity and development. At the beginning of the 20th century, the French anthropologist Claude Levi-Strauss compared São Paulo with Chicago and other great American cities for its ability to reinvent itself.[19] Yet it grew arbitrarily, without a consistent urban strategy, and has been governed by groups that have not been able or willing to formulate a coherent response to urban growth. The impact of this neglect on city residents is evident. As put forth by Gilberto Dimenstein "the self-esteem of *Paulistanos* is so low, that we believe that we're destined to an irreversible urban collapse."[20]

In contrast to São Paulo, the residents of Curitiba, who in the past suffered from an inferiority complex due to the city's lack of infrastructure and the perception that it would simply remain a provincial big town, now have a much improved view of their city, and its national reputation has grown. A majority of respondents in a 2001 national public poll cited the capital of Paraná as the place where they would like to live.[21] *Curitibanos* have developed a healthy obsession with the idea of maintaining what the city has achieved, and there is active public involvement in decisions about the future of the metropolis. Probably like almost nowhere else in Brazil, the notion of "thinking the city" is quite often heard in Curitiba, and it means to plan for the future and to avoid the traps of uncontrolled urbanization. *Curitibanos* believe they have to be vigilant and keep their government on track.

Despite the successes that have been achieved, Curitiba is not a model city or urban utopia. The city itself, with a population of 1.8 million, is at the center of a sprawling metropolitan region with 26 autonomous municipalities and 3.5 million residents. The area has experienced one of the fastest growth rates in the country, and it is one of the main final destinations for peasants escaping rural poverty. However, through a governance strategy that has guided urban development for decades, Curitiba, as stated by Peter Evans, has found imaginative ways to attack the problem of livability, whereas other Brazilian cities remain unable to cope with it.[22] Curitiba's evolution shows the benefits of integrative public planning as government intervention has altered and improved the city's physical and socioeconomic profile.

THE URBAN POLITICAL ECONOMY

During the colonial period the south of Brazil was largely neglected; neither Curitiba, established in 1693 by a group of Portuguese colonists, nor São Paulo, founded by Jesuits in 1554, were considered jewels of the crown. The bulk of economic activity in the colony, especially mining, sugar plantations, and the slave trade, was concentrated in the northeast, where the initial large urban settlements included the city of Salvador, the capital of colonial Brazil, and Recife. Although independence in 1822 transferred political power to Rio de Janeiro, the new nation's capital, São Paulo, Curitiba, and Porto Alegre were to remain dusty and sleepy provincial towns without influence for several decades. Only in the first half of the 20th century did São Paulo became South America's largest industrial center, incurring severe urban problems along the way. Curitiba, however, only started to show signs of urban saturation in the 1960s. When the country's political climate changed radically with the military coup in 1964, the city had 400,000 inhabitants and was absolutely unprepared to cope with the socioeconomic changes caused by the accelerated process of urbanization and the push for industrialization.

Although Curitiba was still an industrial laggard in the mid-1960s, especially compared to São Paulo, both cities suffered from overburdened and inadequate mass transit systems. Urban experts agree that means of transportation are much more than mere connections between home and work. By enabling city dwellers to assimilate pieces of the urban space, public transportation promotes social cohesion and integrates residents into city life.[23] In Curitiba, the city center was permanently congested because most buses passed through downtown even if their origin and destination were in the periphery. São Paulo's transit system was tortured by a chaotic road design, which did not take into consideration the city's hills-valley-hills topography. Beyond design issues, transit quality was abysmal as bus companies faced uncertain investment returns. Old and uncomfortable vehicles increased travel times and caused long delays at bus stops.

Both cities also experienced problems with flooding. In Curitiba, the conversion of rivers into canals was done without adequate consideration of the need for drainage. Flooding remains a chronic affliction for São Paulo residents to this day, a situation worsening by high levels of water pollution. The river Tamanduateí has been compared to a sewage canal, as it receives the waste from thousands of residents and has not been treated for decades. By the 1990s, a prestigious privately owned radio station launched an educational campaign—Save the Tietê—in hopes of forcing the government to act and rescue that river. Yet at the dawn of the 21st century, none of São Paulo's major rivers, the Tietê, the Pinheiros, and the Tamanduateí, have been saved though not for a lack of proposals. Wilheim and other urban planners had presented several plans to São Paulo's government to improve the rivers' condition, enhance the valleys where they are situated, and put in place land use regulations that could combat the flooding problem. Four decades later, despite the warnings made by urban experts about the disarray that was strangling São Paulo, the economically and politically mighty metropolis remains without a coherent urban policy. The lack of a blueprint to deal with the challenges posed by a metropolis that generates a considerable portion of the country's GDP has produced only confusing government responses to the city's most pressing problems.[24]

Hopes for better provision of public services in Brazilian cities were heightened in 1985 when the military relinquished power after 21 years. The country embarked on an ebullient democratic transition, and in 1988 a new constitution was promulgated. There were expectations that the new powers conferred to local governments through the process of political, fiscal, and administrative decentralization would make city halls more accountable and responsive.[25] Yet while local governments were empowered by the legitimacy conferred by popular vote and the addition of new financial resources, the results in terms of service delivery and public sector efficacy have been largely disappointing. So far the transfer of power from national to subnational levels of government has not been matched by an expansion of local responsibilities. There is evidence that a great number of local public officials, largely unprepared to assume new tasks, are using their autonomy to foster private interests. Although convincing data about improvements in public spending and service delivery are scant, some estimates indicate that about 60% of the revenue transferred from the federal to the subnational level is not linked to any specific municipal project.[26]

Decentralization has also had a negative impact on local legislatures to the detriment of municipal governance strategies. Strengthened by the new constitution, city councils have become enormous drains on local resources "as a result of a perverse combination of inefficiency, employment haven, and corruption."[27] A study of 5,507 municipalities produced by the Ministry of Treasury concluded that as a common practice, city councilmen do not hesitate to appropriate for themselves about 10–15% of the municipal budget. In some cases, the amount misused is larger than that allocated to health, education, and public work. Moreover, the city size does not appear to be related to the misuse of public money. The study reported, for instance, widespread corruption in Chã-Grande, one of the smallest towns in the impoverished northeast, as well as in São Paulo. The presence of different mafias operating in Brazil's largest city, with the involvement of a group of councilmen, is a well-known fact.

Setting aside the issue of its effects on local government performance, democracy has clearly benefited Brazil. People are now free to choose their leaders, and through the tools provided by a constitutional and representative democracy, public officials are turned out of office by either elections or impeachment. Political opponents are no longer jailed and tortured as they were in the past. The Brazilian press, one of the most mature in Latin America, is free and is no longer strangled by a state censorship system. In fact, in the last 20 years, the print and electronic media have become an effective voice against government misdeeds. Brazilians enjoy freedom of expression and assembly, and can freely subscribe to a labor union or political party; they can travel to Cuba without being harassed by the Federal Police (as they were in the past). Living under a constitution that is considered one of most progressive in the world (and for that reason it is seen, by some, unworkable in many aspects), Brazilians can sue any governmental institution.

The list of benefits could go on. Nonetheless, whereas democratic consolidation in Brazil has the potential to change state-society relations, the existence of a causal relationship between democratic politics and improved government performance cannot be automatically assumed.[28] It is not necessarily the case that a democratic government will improve the delivery of public services because people in positions of power are not always willing to adopt better governance strategies.[29] As a result of democratization and decentralization, Brazilian municipal governments have expanded their financial capabilities, but this has occurred without a clear improvement in government performance. In several cases, politically empowered mayors have succumbed to the temptations created by increased amounts of financial resources flowing to city hall. The result has been that a large number of cities are still deprived of basic services. Thanks to democracy, citizens can get rid of bad politicians but there is no guarantee that more responsible ones will replace them. In the last 10 years, a solid body of literature has documented instances of poor performance by Brazil's public institutions and prompted scholars to seek explanations as to why the return of democracy has not produced improvements in governance at any level.[30]

CITY PROGRAMS

Public transportation and environmental management—the two government programs under examination in this book—have been chosen as the appropriate topics for policy analysis because they put social needs and demands face to face with government response. Because of their ramifications for human well-being and natural resources conservation, public transportation and environmental management have profound human, social, and economic impacts. A 1999 comprehensive comparative study conducted by Roger-Mark de Souza, focusing on the relationship between housing and transportation patterns in Mexico City, Bangkok, and Washington, DC, shows how inadequacies in mass transit pose threats to human health and the environment. In cities where large segments of the low-income population live in the periphery—Mexico City is one case—precarious transportation systems produce a clear negative outcome on human well-being. Under these circumstances, the urban poor feel isolated and have limited access to employment and recreation facilities, which are generally located in the city center. Low-income groups spend a large percentage of their salaries on public transportation, which leaves them with less family money available for education and health care.

The 1988 Brazilian constitution attributes, albeit in loose ways, several functions and responsibilities to city halls. For example, city governments are entitled to develop policy for local public transportation and environmental management. Yet it is important to note that even during the authoritarian regime (1964–1985), city governments were not completely deprived of the ability to act on urban development matters. Mayors did have room to maneuver, provided they followed the urban directives contained in the military-sponsored II PND (National Development Plan). One of the most consequential of those directives was the establishment of several metropolitan regions in 1974, in which the military sought to exercise territorial control in response to the growing urban crisis in the country. The PND document acknowledged that distortions in the urbanization process were causing traffic jams, overpopulation, and pollution; all these created a negative impact on quality of life and social harmony.

By the time the II PND was implemented in the mid-1970s, there was already evidence indicating that public transportation services in both large and small cities were overwhelmingly inadequate in terms of capacity, routes, and comfort. Three decades later, conditions have not changed substantially. In fact, a comprehensive radiography of the sector, produced by the National Association of Urban Transportation, asserts that mass transportation in Brazil is experiencing one of the worst crises in its history as evidenced by poor road infrastructure and the poor quality of service provided to the people. The study emphasizes that transportation problems that were previously confined to metropolitan areas are spreading to other urban centers, and have a negative impact on the quality of life and the urban economy. Moreover, even though public transportation is identified in the country's constitution as an essential service, the report finds that public policies exert much emphasis on individual means of travel instead of mass transportation.[31]

Brazilian society is paying a heavy toll as a result of the deterioration of mass transit. For the almost 60 million passengers who rely daily on the service, the cost in terms of long journeys, discomfort, and endless delays is enormous. It is also clear that the decay hits the urban poor particularly hard as buses are their principal mode of transportation. At the same time, the unreliable public transportation system also affects the middle class by increasing their use of cars, which contributes to traffic jams and longer commuting times. Traffic congestion also has a well-known detrimental impact on the environment. Marcos Bicalho, a public transportation expert, has been a vocal critic of what he calls the public sector omission. In a 1998 study he argued that by disregarding this essential service, authorities reveal a lack of understanding of the vital role played by public transportation in relation to the urban economy and the population's welfare. His view is that in countries such as Brazil, where a powerful business class operates bus services, government action is absolutely indispensable to reconcile disparate interests. Government is needed to serve as a bridge between the demands for profit (transportation as an economic activity) and the needs for service delivery (transportation as social policy).

Environmental degradation is one of the great challenges faced by urban governments. It poses a constant threat to human well-being, and it is increasingly becoming a liability

to economic development. In a fine analysis of the
relationship between urban centers and the environment,
William Rees and Mathis Wackernagel in 1996 very well
addressed the problem by asking "why cities cannot be sustainable and why they are a key to sustainability." Public
policies implemented to develop the local economy and
make cities the loci of progress are often detrimental to
the environment. Most city governments find it a daunting challenge to manage the environmental protection ver-
sus economic growth equation. However, it is plausible to
assume that urban centers facing environmental decay with
high pollution levels and inadequate sanitation systems are
likely to be less attractive to the business community.

Serious concerns about the negative effects of urbanization
and the issue of urban sustainability emerged during the
early 1990s, and since then the fate of cities worldwide has
been the central theme of major international meetings.[32]
As a result, a consensus has grown around the idea that no
development path is sustainable if it relies on the depletion
of nonrenewable natural resources. Societies can only be
called sustainable if they pass on an undiminished amount
of resources from one generation to the next.[33] In practice,
however, urban sustainability has proved to be rather an
elusive goal. City governments find it difficult, if not impossible, to adopt and coordinate a set of policies that accommodate economic development and environmental quality.
The challenge is partly the result of the multiplicity of issues
involved in the sustainability equation, as environmental
protection is related to sanitation, more efficient modes of
public transportation, pollution control, natural resources

preservation, garbage collection, and public awareness.[34] The difficulties governments encounter in trying to coordinate these policy areas raise a legitimate question of whether cities can contribute to sustainable development. Be that as it may, urban centers are being called on to take the lead. The final conclusions that emerged from the 1992 Earth Summit argue that "if sustainable development does not start in the cities, it simply will not go. Cities have got to lead the way."[35]

The environmental management record in Brazilian metropolitan areas is not very encouraging. Many cities struggle with air pollution levels, uncontrolled floods, water problems, and serious inadequacies in garbage disposal. The problems are aggravated by society's lack of information regarding both environmental and health risks, despite numerous studies by development agencies such as the World Bank that link human contact with contaminated wastewater to high rates of infant mortality. In addition to the direct impact waste management programs could have on public health, there are potential social benefits to such programs in terms of job creation for the urban poor. Yet local governmental response within Brazil has been timid and beset with policy discontinuities. Municipal authorities are charged with responsibilities for garbage collection, recycling, street cleaning, and preservation of public spaces. Yet despite their constitutional obligations, it is still relatively common for cities to engage in the practice of dumping solid waste on vacant lands. Beyond the obvious health hazards, this type of government neglect represents a missed opportunity to increase the efficiency of urban resources and to promote economic development, as the recycling of urban waste can be the basis for new city businesses.

Likewise, local governments in Brazil have paid little attention to the betterment of urban environments. Contrary to the misconceived notion that trees are just a cosmetic remedy to urban blight, the arborization of urban areas has important positive outcomes such as the reduction of cooling costs and the diminishment of noise.[36] A consensus seems to be growing regarding the relevance of green areas, wooded city parks, and urban forests. In the United States, there are at least 2,700 heads of local governments committed to the creation and preservation of urban forests. The mayors' rationale derives from a belief that the vitality of communities is strongly dependent on the quality of the city's green spaces. In a document submitted to the US Congress—"Community and Urban Forestry Resolution"— the mayors even noted that open green spaces and tree-sheltered streets alleviate the mental fatigue associated with urban life.[37] Along these lines, David Satterthwaite, who has written extensively about urban pressures in the developing world, asserts that green areas are critical for the improvement of urban environments. Planting trees in cities, he says "cannot only be justified for their aesthetic value, but also for their contribution to, among other things, reducing cooling costs, absorbing pollutants and acting as windbreaks and noise barriers.[38]

Without being the perfect or ultimate response to the problems facing Brazil's cities, the Curitiba case is an example of a more positive and effective approach to governance, one which produced results even when local public officials were constrained by the moderate-to-strong level of centralization imposed by military rulers. The urban development process in Curitiba also demonstrates the self-reinforcing nature of policy environments as posited by the path-dependent model. Initially, the public entrepreneurial attitude displayed by the governing group contributed to the emergence of a new policy environment, which would prove critical in the end in the process of urban reform in Curitiba. Once public officials committed themselves to a course of action and positive results emerged, it became easier for subsequent governments to adhere to the same governance strategy. Consistency tempered with the requisite flexibility produced successful outcomes. Far from envisioning a utopian city, those behind the Curitiba master plan were looking to shape a more livable metropolis through a sensible set of government actions to ensure that urban growth would not deteriorate city living.

ENDNOTES

1. Ruy Barbosa de Oliveira (1849–1923). Brazilian lawyer, journalist and politician; a federal representative, senator, a minister for taxation, diplomat and a candidate for presidency of the Republic. For his participation in the Hague Conventions (1899 and 1907), and in the peace conference in The Hague (1907), he earned the nickname of the "Eagle of the Hague."
2. A study of Warsaw, Rome, and Stockholm, 2002.
3. Lefebvre (1969, 1996) discussed the rights of residents to make use of the urban space in its entirety, independently of social class and legal status. Several authors have since interpreted Lefebvre's work. Purcell (2005), for instance, has argued that Lefebvre's concept of the right to the city encompasses the right to determine how the urban space is produced. In Purcell's view, democratization of urban politics is not confined to access to public services, but the citizens' ability to "decide the geography of public space." Harvey (2003) offered another interpretation of Lefebvre by arguing that the right to the city "is not merely a right to access what already exists, but a right to change it after our heart's desire."
4. At present, international development agencies, such as the Habitat International Coalition (2005), define the "right to the city" as "the equitable usufruct of cities considering the principles of sustainability and social justice" This modern version of Lefebvre's "right to the city" seeks to promote equal access to the potential benefits of the city to all urban dwellers and that urban residents may fully realize their fundamental rights and liberties.
5. Elkin and Soltan (1993).
6. Path—dependence, as explained by Pierson (2004), predicts that institutions are self reinforcing: once a course of action is taken, it becomes more difficult to change it.
7. Cited in *New Frontiers in Urban Governance* (2000, p. 13).
8. A detailed account of urban reforms in the United States is presented by Holli (1999).
9. As explained by Pierson (1999) and Sewell (1996).

10. See Yates (1977).
11. See Schneider and Tesk (1995, p. 3).
12. See Fried and Rabinovitz (1980, p. 66).
13. See Ferreira (1999). Also, data provided by the Brazilian Institute of Geography and Statistics show that the most important reasons for people to join unions are access to health plans and sport/recreation facilities. Joining a labor union for political reasons ranks low: while union membership was associated to politics in 7.4% of people interviewed in metropolitan areas in 1988, the figure dropped to 2.3% in 1996.
14. Roberts and King (1991).
15. As cited in *VEJA*. See Traumman (1999).
16. Eaton (2006) provides an interesting account of the ways in which military governments in Brazil promoted subnational institutions by expanding the policy tools at disposal of local governments.
17. In 1968 during Mayor Faria Lima's term, another one in 1971 under Mayor Reynaldo de Barros, and in 1988 a new master plan was designed during the Jânio Quadros administration. At the time of this writing, São Paulo was again experimenting with a new master plan, approved by the city council in 2002.
18. Romero (2000).
19. Levi-Strauss' impressions on urban life in Brazil are in *Tristes Tropiques*. In the 1930s he taught at the University of São Paulo.
20. Cited by Romero (2000).
21. Poll conducted by the Institute for Social, Political and Economic Research (IPESPE), as cited in *VEJA*, January 31, 2001, p. 29.
22. According to the definition by Washington-based Worldwatch Institute, livability merges economic viability, social cohesiveness, and environmental health.
23. Wilheim (1965).
24. In 2002 the São Paulo City Council approved a new urban planning instrument authored by Jorge Wilheim, and later modified by local legislators. Soon after, controversy emerged regarding the implementation of the plan's directives.
25. Fiscal decentralization in Brazil includes transfers (grants) from the federal government to the states, and federal and state grants to the municipalities. According to the Constitution, the federal government

is required to transfer to the states 21.5% of the federal tax revenues and from the industrial products tax (IPI). Another 22.5% of the federal income tax, the IPI is distributed to municipal governments, from which 10% is transferred to the state capitals, among them Curitiba and São Paulo; the remaining 90% goes to all other municipalities. The state governments collect a value added tax and are required to transfer 25% of the proceeds to city governments within their respective jurisdictions. Municipal governments also collect their own taxes on property (IPTU) and on services (ISS).

26. As cited in Willis, Garman and Haggard (1999). The authors provide an extensive analysis of decentralization policies in Argentina, Mexico, Brazil, Colombia, and Venezuela.
27. Reported by Dieguez (2000).
28. Similar results were achieved by Moreno-Jaimes (2007) in his study of municipal governments in Mexico. His most important conclusion is that "electoral democracy in Mexico has not yet implied better-quality governments, a finding that casts serious doubts on the ability of elections to serve, by themselves, as instruments to promote the responsiveness of local governments…at least in terms of policy efficacy."
29. Another illustrative case is Bolivia, as demonstrated by McNeish (2006).
30. Among them Weyland, *Democracy Without Equity: Failures of Reform in Brazil*; Schneider, *Brazil: Culture and Politics in a New Industrial Powerhouse*; Hagopian, *Traditional Politics and Regime Change in Brazil*; Souza, *Constitutional Engineering in Brazil: The Politics of Federalism and Decentralization*. See also Galeano, *Upside Down* for insights into democracy's pitfalls in Latin America.
31. See *Desoneração dos Custos e Barateamento das Tarifas do Trasnporte Público*. Associação Nacional das Empresas de Transportes Urbanos, March 2006.
32. For example, the Earth Summit or Rio 92 (United Nations Conference on Environment and Development; the City Summit (Habitat I), UN sponsored, held in Montreal in 1976; Habitat II, held in Istanbul in 1996.
33. As cited in Daily and Ehrlich (1992).
34. Based on a comparative study of environmental institutions in Curitiba and Colombian cities by Tlayie and Biller (1994).

35. As cited in Brugmann (1996).
36. See Satterthwaite (1998) for a comprehensive picture of the relevance of green areas in urban centers.
37. There have been several other green initiatives in the United States. In New York City, for instance, the city hall and city council reached an agreement in 2002 to preserve 400 urban gardens. See also Fazio (2002).
38. Satterthwaite (1998, p. 88).

CHAPTER 2

COPING WITH
URBAN PROBLEMS

Clearly there is no single answer to the question of how to
maintain urban amenities and keep cities—where most people will soon live—functioning and tolerable. It will take a
combination of a great many measures that inspire individual responsibility, social will, and economic innovation. No
doubt "quality leadership" is a key factor, and people must
be able to find where to look for it.

—Flora Lewis[1]

The political economy of rapidly growing cities in many
developing countries generally presents a challenging profile. The needs created by fast-paced urbanization and large
population inflows often overmatch the financial resources,

physical infrastructure, technical expertise, political will, and organizational capacity available to the policymakers and officials charged with governance. Against this backdrop, Curitiba's success in creating a more coherent policy environment for addressing urban problems has been a remarkable accomplishment. This chapter examines that achievement in relation to two fundamental urban issues: public transportation and environmental management.

URBAN MOBILITY IN CURITIBA

Curitiba's mass transit now serves as a global model for sustainable transportation policies. The city's success in this area raises a number of questions. How were local authorities in Curitiba able to rescue and redefine the city's transportation system, a task that remains a major challenge for other city governments in Brazil? Why was public transportation made a government priority in the Paraná state capital, and how has the commitment been sustained?

The much-improved status of the public transportation network today, acknowledged by several experts,[2] is in striking contrast with the sad state of affairs that existed in the 1960s. Prior to implementation of the *Plano Diretor* in 1965, a city hall assessment made public by the local newspaper *Gazeta do Povo* identified Curitiba's public transportation system as erratic, unreliable, and near collapse. Bus trips within the city suffered from long delays and increased travel times. According to an expert report:

> The city did not have a transportation system. Rather it had a collection of mismatched con-

cessions granted to private companies. There were few guidelines to encourage transportation firms to provide effective service to the city as whole. The city simply assigned an exclusive area of operation to each company within the municipality. Transportation evolved in reaction to the location of commercial, industrial, and residential activities rather than in concert with them. Transportation companies operated without competition within their concessions. They ignored districts with medium and low demographic densities and, when route schedules did exist, did not enforce them. Bus routes merely linked origin and destination pairs within the city. The city center was typically one element in these pairs. The confluence of routes in the central city increased central traffic congestion. Transfers between routes required a payment of a second fare. The necessity of transfers increased queuing and travel times.[3]

The first stage of Curitiba's new transportation policies began in 1964 under the administration of Mayor Ivo Arzua as a result of his decision to revamp the urban space. The city government received several urban planning proposals and awarded a contract to the São Paulo-based architectural firm Serete (*Sociedade de Estudos e Projetos*). Jorge Wilheim, an expert in city affairs, was the firm's chief architect and was already well known for his attempts to convince São Paulo's authorities to adopt a coherent urban strategy for Brazil's largest city. A preliminary urban plan was drawn that eventually resulted in the *Plano Diretor de Curitiba*, the city master plan, which is still in effect today. The master plan conceived a new urban model, in which mass transit, land use and road systems would be used as tools toward an integrative urban development process.[4] However, it was not easy for the mayor to get city council approval for the new plan. The recent military coup had interrupted the democratic process in Brazil and created a highly politicized climate at the local level. Mayor Arzua realized that he needed public support to get the plan accepted, and so he initiated an educational campaign in which he made several visits personally to neighborhoods to explain the master plan's features and implications.

The city government also organized a series of seminars—"Curitiba of Tomorrow"—to promote public debates on the urban planning process. Held over a period of several months between 1964 and 1965, the meetings engaged architects, engineers, sociologists, economists, professors, and journalists in discussions about the city's conditions and what the experts were envisioning for its future. These events took place during a time when the country was experiencing sweeping transformations. Brazil's military rulers pushed the country toward rapid industrialization, and millions of people were literally expelled from rural areas to the major cities, especially to the state capitals. Curitiba was one of the magnets and for three decades, it experienced one of the highest rates of population growth among the largest capital cities, as shown in Table 1.

In retrospect, Arzua's initiative to take urban planning proposals to the streets proved to be critical for city politics in the subsequent years. The public debates, the public relations campaign, and the press coverage of the proposed

Table 1. Urban population growth percentages in Brazil, 1970–2000.

State Capitals	1970–1980	1980–1991	1991–1996	1996–2000
Belém	3.98	2.49	–1.67	2.85
Fortaleza	4.37	2.55	2.17	2.17
Recife	1.36	0.40	0.75	1.40
Salvador	4.07	2.79	1.31	2.52
Belo Horizonte	3.80	0.93	0.73	1.71
Rio de Janeiro	1.85	0.50	0.28	1.35
São Paulo	3.69	1.04	0.44	1.48
Curitiba	5.34	2.29	2.34	1.83
Porto Alegre	2.52	0.79	0.40	1.36
Brazil	2.48	1.93	1.36	1.97

Source. IBGE (1996); IBGE National Census 1970—2000.

master plan planted the roots of a new culture among city residents and influenced the perceptions of politicians and voters about the value of urban development. After Arzua, all mayors, both those who were appointed and those who were elected after the return of democracy, publicly renewed the original commitment to the urban planning process with projects that would enhance programs that were working for the benefit of the city.

The formation of the Institute of Research and Urban Planning of Curitiba (IPPUC) in 1965 helped strengthen the nascent institutional framework in support of the city's development. Although initially seen as one more meaningless municipal agency, the IPPUC in fact soon became a critical tool for the government in terms of both its effect on policy design and its influence on city politics. The IPPUC enjoys considerable autonomy in developing policy proposals for city officials. It provides input at both the early conceptual stages and during application as proposals are implemented. Experts identify the IPPUC as the local incubator of an urban planning process that emphasizes the interplay among planning, analysis, and implementation.[5]

The dynamics between the relevant organizations and the institutional framework in this area recall Douglass North's analysis of institutions and institutional change. As he has observed "both what organizations come into existence and how they evolve are fundamentally influenced by the institutional framework. In turn they influence how the institutional framework evolves." North goes further explaining that in the process of pursuing their objectives organizations alter the institutional structure.[6]

In 1969, Curitiba's government, under Mayor Omar Sabbag, developed its first preliminary mass transit plan in accordance with the master plan. However, it was not until 1971, with the appointment of new mayor Jaime Lerner that the new public transportation system started to take shape. Lerner was a young architect who had worked for the IPPUC, and his commitment to the master plan was immediately made evident with his first initiatives, which were in stark opposition to the urbanization process taking place in the rest of the country. Governments in the largest Brazilian cities were giving clear preference to the car as a means of transportation by building viaducts, bridges, and elevated freeways within the central areas. Curitiba's city hall determined instead that the downtown would be free of cars, and as a result, the country's first pedestrian network was built with several streets reserved for walking. This set the stage for a major revamping of the transit and transportation systems. As part of this process, Lerner reached out to form a partnership with the private bus companies.

Significant changes began in 1974 with the construction of a new road hierarchy within the city and the establishment of strict land use controls. Five arterial roads were built as triple driving systems: in each, a central road with two restricted lanes dedicated to express buses is flanked by two local roads that allow fast car circulation in and out of the city center. The system has grown incrementally with the addition of new bus lines and new bus services. The road hierarchy now includes priority linkage roads connecting the city center to the periphery, connector streets linking the industrial area to the structural roads and collector streets allowing all forms of traffic.

Although enhancements in Curitiba's transportation system have been a priority for successive governments, public officials have had to overcome a number of significant technical, political, and administrative obstacles throughout the system's incremental development and expansion. In the beginning, there were problems with route design and a need for better vehicles. Contracts with the bus companies had to be established with clear rules regarding fares, revenue sharing, and bus schedules. Although the IPPUC has been an integral part of the institutional framework guiding the development of transportation policy, the monitoring and enforcement of standards in mass transit is within another municipal agency, Urbanização Curitiba—URBS—which has pioneered software for bus timetables, a truly innovative and helpful management tool that has been transferred from Curitiba to other capital cities.

Officially known as the Curitiba Integrated Transportation Network (RIT), the city's bus system offers a rich mix of services, including high-capacity buses operating on designated roads, orbital routes that interconnect the bus lines, and limited-stop high-speed buses. This variety has led urban planning experts such as Robert Cervero (1995) to identify Curitiba's public transportation system as one of the most innovative to date. In fact, more than 30 years after its creation, the Curitiba mass transportation network is recognized internationally for its efficiency. Known by policymakers as "bus rapid transit," the system seems to be a better option than underground trains for transporting millions of riders everyday.[7] The main features of Curitiba's mass transit system, as described by Rabinovitch and Hoehn in 1995, are summarized in Table 2.

Public surveys conducted by local authorities and international development agencies indicate a high degree of satisfaction with the Curitiba mass transit system. It has been reported, for instance, that 95% of bus riders who had visited other Brazilian capital cities rated Curitiba's system higher for its degree of comfort and travel time.[8]

Tables 3–5 provide additional comparative information on the performance of Curitiba's transportation services.

Table 2. The Curitiba mass transit system.

Main Routes

Express Routes
Buses circulate on the structural roads and run independently of car traffic. This allows the core system to be free of traffic jams at peak times, increasing the comfort and speed of travel.

Direct Routes
Buses run in parallel with the structural corridors. All direct buses use the boarding tube stations, which are equipped with special lifts for wheelchairs, strollers, and people with special transportation needs.

Inter-district Routes
Buses make orbital trips between the direct and structural express routes. They link many neighborhoods without going to the city center. Inter-district routes allow transfers to the express, direct, and feeder routes.

Feeder Routes
Buses circulate within residential areas linking them to transfer terminals. Currently, there are 111 feeder routes in operation.

Conventional Routes
Buses run from specific neighborhoods to the city center. There are 96 conventional routes in operation.

City Center Routes
Minibuses with a 40-passenger capacity circulate only around city center in a clockwise and counterclockwise system. The service is ideal for shoppers and other people who need to make short trips within downtown Curitiba.

Neighborhood Routes
Minibuses that circulate exclusively within specific neighborhoods.

Night Routes
Buses circulate from 1 to 5 a.m. at 1-hour intervals between each vehicle.

(continued)

Table 2. The Curitiba mass transit system (*continued*).

Electric Tramway

This is the most recent addition to the system. At present, electrical vehicles are circulating only on the structural corridors. The greatest advantage is the substitution of cleaner electric power for diesel fuel.

Pro-Park Routes

Three lines connecting downtown to the city parks.

Vehicles

Minibuses for small routes and fast trips
Padron buses with a capacity of 110 passengers
Articulated buses for up to 170 passengers
Biarticulated buses and high capacity for 270 passengers

Bus Terminals

Currently, there are 268 boarding tube stations (*estações tubo*), one of the system's most significant innovations. The station is a tube-shaped aluminum and glass structure that lies parallel to the road. Embarking passengers enter the tube, pass a turnstile, pay the fare, and wait for the bus on an elevated platform at the same level as the bus. When the vehicle aligns itself with the boarding tube, the bus driver, through a remote control system, opens the doors of the bus and the tube. Without stairs to climb, passengers embark and disembark quickly using different doors. Swift boarding times reduce travel times and increase the capacity of the system.

Transfer Terminals

There are 25 enclosed structures, which work like surface subway stations. Passengers are free to walk inside the terminals, make phone calls, and buy newspapers. People who disembark from a bus can change to another one without having to pay another fare.

Single Fare

Bus passengers are allowed to make unlimited connections within the system with only one ticket. (In other cities, passengers have to pay a fare each time they board a bus.)

Special Services

The transportation system in Curitiba also performs special educational and social functions. Buses in the city run for no more than 10 years.

(*continued*)

Table 2. The Curitiba mass transit system (*continued*).

After that, the city government recycles them into mobile training centers for computing, electrical repair, and other courses. The municipality pays the instructors, and the buses park in different low-income neighborhoods on scheduled days of the week. About 20,000 people have graduated from this job-training program since it started in 1991.

New Bus Design
Curitiba inaugurated a new era of mass transit vehicles in Brazil, where buses had been assembled over a truck chassis, had small doors and steep, narrow stairways, and were noisy and bumpy. As part of the process of revamping the public transportation system, Curitiba officials negotiated with Volvo to manufacture new buses with three wider doors, lower floor levels, and rear engines, which reduce weight and noise. This action by the Curitiba government has helped to develop quality standards and a market for Brazilian urban buses.

Table 3. Bus system performance in selected Brazilian cities.

State Capitals	Passenger Journeys Per Capita[1]	Fleet Buses/1,000 Inhabitants[2]	Route km/1,000 Per Capita[3]
Fortaleza	184	0.61	0.96
Porto Alegre	120	0.58	n.a.
São Paulo	158	0.66	4.09
Curitiba	202	0.97	0.76

Source. Rabinovitch and Hoehn (1995) and Bushell (1993).
Notes. [1]Residents are more likely to use a transportation system when it offers convenience and speed. The desire to use mass transit is best measured by annual per capita use, that is, the annual number of trips taken in a city divided by the city's population.
[2]A high number of buses per capita is correlated with high per capita use.
[3]Shorter routes mean that a given number of vehicles may provide more frequent service, even if the number of kilometers traveled by the buses declines.

Table 4. Fuel lost as a result of severe traffic congestion—selected state capitals.

City	Fuel Losses (R$ Million/Year)*
Belo Horizonte	4.54
Curitiba	1.98
Porto Alegre	2.06
Rio de Janeiro	28.65

Source. CNT (2002, p. 42).
Note. *R$ (Real) represents the Brazilian currency. 1 Real = US$ 0.47 (2006).

Table 5. Cost of time lost as a result of severe traffic congestion—selected state capitals.

City	Cost of Time Lost (R$ Million/Year)*
Belo Horizonte	20.19
Curitiba	2.55
Porto Alegre	2.82
Rio de Janeiro	8.46

Source. CNT (2002, p. 23).
Note. *R$ (Real) represents the Brazilian currency. 1 Real = US$ 0.47 (2006).

The partnership between the public and private sectors has been a crucial aspect both in the development and implementation of Curitiba's transportation system. In contrast to São Paulo, where for decades the two sectors have been in competition over the provision of transportation services, bus routes in Curitiba have always been in private hands. However, for decades the service was chaotic and inefficient. It was only after the master plan was approved and transportation proposals were developed that the city government began to regulate the operations of the private bus companies.

The reasons why bus owners—a conservative group and resistant to change—agreed with city hall regulations will be discussed in the following chapters. It suffices to say for now that based on IPPUC studies, city hall was able to negotiate a deal with the bus owners by establishing an innovative revenue fare system. Under this arrangement, financial compensation for each company is based on the number of kilometers traveled by vehicle type and the percentage of compliance it achieves in meeting route timetables. Each firm has a specific schedule and number of kilometers per route. Companies do not receive revenues according to numbers of passengers— an increase in ridership does not increase compensation for the private firms. Instead, companies have a financial incentive to increase their "on time" compliance with the set route schedules. Through these criteria, the government ensures not only that people have access to transportation but also that quality standards are in place, especially in terms of schedules, routes, and punctuality.

The operation is monitored and enforced by URBS under plans elaborated by the IPPUC. URBS is in charge of the revenue-sharing program, negotiates contracts with private bus companies, administers the bus terminals, and monitors the performance of the system. Although only URBS can sign transportation contracts, the city government may cancel permits to a bus company at any time when standards and conditions are not met. A 1990 law also stipulates that the government will reimburse bus companies according to the number of scheduled kilometers that they actually travel.

Adopted incrementally and in accordance with city growth and city needs, the transportation system has not evolved without conflict. The bus companies constantly exert pressure on the government for higher fares; at the same time, passengers often demand lower fares. It appears, however, that the quality of service has been the main card in the hands of governments to reconcile such disparate interests. Constant improvements in public transportation have helped public officials to convince city residents that "there is a price to pay" for good service; at the same time, by providing physical and administrative infrastructure (system management, terminals, lighting, stations, and paved roads), the city government contributes to the firms' profitability, thereby helping to reduce the pressure for higher fares.

Different cities have different requirements for a mass transit system and these variations are significant enough to avoid the temptation to declare that Curitiba's transportation system should be a model for other metropolises. Yet whereas it may not be possible or desirable to replicate a given mass transit system in another city, the governance strategies in Curitiba might be applicable elsewhere. In the case of public transportation, Curitiba's governments have acted to improve bus service in ways that were not isolated from other aspects of urban life. Instead of being captive to a static planning process, which soon becomes outdated due to the dynamism of large cities, Curitiba's governments have adhered to the original master plan but incorporated changes to meet new objectives. For example, as new transportation routes were put into place, the city also developed low-income housing projects near these transportation corridors. Infrastructure for new roads led to programs to control flooding, and a public campaign to convince residents to leave their cars at home and ride the bus also had the objective of increasing environmental awareness. Municipal authorities have also made efforts to diversify modes of transportation within city limits by developing 120 km (74.5 miles) of bicycle routes that allow easy connections among the 25 city parks. Curitiba's bicycle fleet is now estimated at 121,000.[9]

The master plan acquired life with the implementation of innovative road and public transportation systems that are connected to land use patterns. Whereas traditional city planning approaches try, in general, to address physical features, in Curitiba the evolution of the planning process shows that governments have not and do not isolate transportation from other aspects of urban life. According to Rabinovitch and Hoehn, "they do not view streets only as paved surfaces but as elements in a larger network and hierarchy of roads. A building is not an isolated box, but rather a traffic/public transport-generating element in a larger pattern of settlement."[10]

ENVIRONMENTAL MANAGEMENT

Environmental degradation is one of the greatest challenges facing urban governments. Contaminants in the air, water, and soil pose serious threats to human well-being and are increasingly a liability for economic development. Moreover, although the problem seems particularly acute in the troubled large cities in the developing world, urban centers in the developed world also struggle with environmental decay. Satterthwaite, for instance, has stressed that "most governments in the North also continue to view economic growth as the main means by which unemployment is to be reduced and incomes increased and it is difficult if not impossible to combine these with significant falls in the use of non-renewable resources and the generation of greenhouse gases, unless there is an explicit linking of employment generation with such goals."[11]

The tasks confronting urban government are enormous. On the one hand, there is the economic development imperative, dependent on investments, industrial production, and a favorable business climate; on the other, governmental action and measures to build a solid economic basis to make cities the loci of progress are more than often detrimental to resources' conservation. Thus, as they are considered engines for prosperity, cities and the process of urbanization are linked to a global ecological decline. The challenge, therefore, for local governments is how to reconcile economic growth and environmental protection.

The fate of cities has been subject of numerous international fora, in which serious concerns have emerged regarding urbanization and the question of urban sustainability.[12] The reality has demonstrated that city governments find it difficult, if not impossible, to put in practice and coordinate sustainable policies, as they are not confined to a single issue, but a variety of them. In fact, in urban centers, large and small, several factors interfere with the sustainability equation as environmental protection is related to sanitation, more efficient modes of transportation, pollution control, natural resource conservation, and garbage collection. The difficulties confronted by governments to coordinate these policy areas have raised serious questions about the possibility that any city can reach a sustainable status. At the same time, if we take sustainability as a process, and not an outcome, our thinking about the role of cities may change: instead of black holes, they could take, in fact, the vanguard of the movement toward sustainable development.[13]

According to Pedro Jacobi, one of Brazil's most authoritative scholars on urban sustainability, environmental problems are increasing in the country's metropolitan areas. He speaks of a "permanent degradation," which is most visible in the high pollution levels, uncontrolled floods, and serious inadequacies in garbage treatment that are prevalent in Brazil's cities. For Jacobi, the problems are aggravated by a societal lack of information and awareness regarding the environmental and health risks associated with the situation. He criticizes timid governmental initiatives and policy discontinuities that have had the effect of "creat[ing] a truly vicious circle based on the logic of blaming the victim."[14]

Within the broad field of environmental management, this study focuses on two specific issues: garbage collection (including waste recycling) and the creation of wooded city parks. They were selected for two major reasons: first, they are among the municipal responsibilities detailed in Brazil's

1988 federal constitution; and, second, these are programs that international organizations, such as the United Nations and urban experts, emphasize as being important for human well-being, urban sustainability, and local development.

A number of United Nations and World Bank studies have emphasized that water contaminated by human waste and household trash is a main cause of infectious diseases linked to high rates of infant mortality. Waste management programs, including recycling, also have a great potential for employment creation and income generation for the poor. One United Nations study[15] has stressed that "promoting the separation by each household of recyclables and organic wastes from the rest of their wastes ensures much higher levels of recycling and safer working conditions for those who collect the recyclables, compared to waste picking." Several experts have emphasized that by neglecting an essential service—garbage collection and recycling—city authorities are wasting opportunities to increase the efficiency of urban resources and to promote economic development, as urban waste can be the basis for new city businesses.[16] Finally, urban green areas, wooded city parks, and wetlands have proven to be effective in reducing the risk of flooding and limiting flood damage, an issue of great concern in both São Paulo and Curitiba.

Unfortunately, it is a common practice in many cities to dump solid waste on vacant land on the outskirts of the city with no preparation of the site to minimize the risk of contaminating nearby water sources. Arguably a very sophisticated metropolis, Rio de Janeiro, is an example of Brazil's municipal governments' inability to manage solid waste.

In the 1990s, more than a quarter of Rio's households did not have a garbage collection service, and sewage was simply dumped untreated into rivers, lakes, and the sea, where it ultimately ended up in the Guanabara Bay, Rio's most famous postcard.[17] Similar situations can be found in many other cities in Brazil and in other Latin American countries. Many local governments have inadequate solid waste management programs and usually only provide garbage collection services to the middle and upper income neighborhoods and the main industrial and commercial areas. According to the United Nations Center for Human Settlements, the lack of sanitation and garbage collection programs "arise[s] largely from a failure of government institutions to manage rapid change and to tap the knowledge, resources and capacities among its population within each city. Indeed, governments have often helped to destroy or stifle the social economy in cities that is so central to their prosperity and to the capacity of the inhabitants in each locality to identify and act on their own priorities."[18]

Curitiba: The Incremental Approach on Environmental Quality

Curitiba is the birthplace of the Iguaçú River, which runs through the far end of the State of Paraná to the border with Paraguay and Argentina. The Itaipú hydroelectric power plant, one of the world's largest, is situated there—as is one of nature's wonders, the Iguaçu Falls. A short distance from the Itaipú reservoir, the Iguaçú becomes a tributary of the Paraná, the one of the world's largest river systems, which is integrated into the Rio de la Plata basin. At its origin in Curitiba, the Iguaçú has several tributaries—the Atuba, Baccheri, Belém, Ivo, Bariguí, and Passaúna. Like the Iguaçú itself, these smaller watercourses cut through long sections of Curitiba's urban area and have also become affected by the garbage and sewage that are the by-products of Curitiba's growing urbanization.

For a long time, however, Curitiba posed no threat to the rivers, and they had no negative effect on the city even during periods of torrential rains and rising waters. It was only in the second half of the 20th century that problems began to emerge as the growing city encroached on the riverbeds and took over the low lands and valley bottoms. The natural consequence was flooding, a plague that affected Curitiba for decades, especially during the austral summer season (December to March), when most of Brazil's south-southeast region experiences heavy rainfall. For successive years, the period between December and March was also a time of great trouble as large stretches of Curitiba were inundated as a result of its rivers overflowing. Until the early 1970s, many conventional engineering works consumed vast amounts of public investments in an attempt to control flooding throughout the low lands of the city. Long sections of Curitiba's rivers were canalized either in underground galleries or in open conduits. However, this strategy did not address the underlying problem, but merely transferred the floodwaters from one place to another. The river dredging that was done only gained about 40 cm in depth, which was insufficient to deal with the volume of water during flooding.

In 1965, a team of city hall planners concluded that a comprehensive urban development program was needed to deal with the flood problem. They came up with an ambitious idea: municipal authorities could intervene to preserve the banks along the rivers and create a series of urban parks as a flood zone that would accommodate periods of heavy rainfall and rising waters. This would require the expropriation of land along the watercourses, construction of small lakes capable of regulating the flow of the Iguaçu and its tributaries and strict regulations governing land use along the river banks. However, at the time this plan was envisioned, the municipal government lacked the financial means to implement it.

Curitiba, along with other major cities and especially the state capitals, was entitled to receive federal money for flood control. Yet the funds were meant for river dredging and concrete canals and not for parks, trees, and lakes. This restriction was an obstacle to dealing with the flooding problem in a comprehensive way until Mayor Lerner took charge in March 1971. Curitiba received funding for yet another conventional engineering approach to the problem, but on receiving the money, the local authorities set aside the original plan and began implementing the earlier design recommendations. Instead of locking up the rivers inside enormous concrete boxes, the new strategy took a much more "natural" approach: areas along the rivers that were subject to flooding were transformed into protected wooded areas where no urban infrastructure could be built.

Between 1971 and 1974, the first two city parks were created—the Bariguí and the São Lourenço on the Belém

River—consisting of a total of 2 million square meters of green areas. Construction was also begun on Iguaçú Park, which at the time of its inauguration in 1982 was Brazil's largest urban green space with 8 million square meters. Later, Iguaçú Park's status was surpassed in size by a park on the Passaúna River, one of the Iguaçú's tributaries. Unlike these others, Passaúna Park was not created to prevent floods. Instead, this huge wooded area (43 million square meters) was intended to ensure the health of the river, the source of one-third of the water Curitiba uses.

From the early practice of using urban parks as flood control zones, Curitiba now has 25 parks in total with estimates of the amount of green area per inhabitant ranging from 20 to 50 square meters (the lower figure is based on independent calculations whereas the higher is a government estimate).[19] Although the underlying reason for the creation of urban parks and wooded areas was not to make Curitiba a greener city, it has had the effect of doing so. The urban park program was developed to address serious environmental problems such as drainage, sanitation, and flood control. However, the parks have also contributed to regulating land use by preventing some central areas from becoming shantytowns.[20] Over time, the policy of protecting wooded areas has increased land prices in affected neighborhoods, to the benefit of real estate and construction firms, and public gardens have been created (and are still in expansion) to increase the city's appeal to tourists. Several of these parks celebrate various immigrant groups such as the Germans, Italians, Poles, and Portuguese who have contributed to the city's development. Moreover, by the late

1980s, as ecological concerns were growing worldwide and the issue of urban sustainability began to make headlines, governments in Curitiba wisely and promptly began incorporating the "green" element in official discourse.

Garbage treatment and disposal has also been a great environmental challenge for Curitiba's governments. The problem is widespread in Brazil, where experts on waste management and its impact on the environment have stressed that the lack of a clear recycling policy undermines many other urban development initiatives. One of these experts, the São Paulo-based economist Sabetai Calderoni, estimates that Brazil as a whole loses an average of US$2 billion annually by not recycling its garbage. He attributes the absence of comprehensive recycling programs at the federal, state, and municipal levels to the lack of a clear, long-term planning vision. In his view, incentives for recycling would lead to gains in energy conservation and reductions in the amount of oil imported for the production of plastics and rubber. Recycling programs would benefit states and municipalities by lowering the costs related to waste management, improving environmental quality, and increasing job creation. Calderoni estimates that the recycling of 1 ton of paper can save 10,000 liters of water and 17 trees.

Until the early 1980s, Curitiba's governments had not taken comprehensive measures to deal with its garbage problems. Commenting on the issue, one of the city's newspapers said of the Belém River, that although it "has been canalized in some parts, yet what remains is dirty water running at open skies, while the banks have become garbage fields."[21] The urban development process initiated in the 1960s, along with the environmental gains produced by the expansion of the mass transit system and the institution of the parks program, helped to build momentum for addressing waste management concerns. Between 1983 and 1985, Mayor Maurício Fruet initiated a twofold municipal initiative that was unique in Brazil at that time. He made the government more accessible to city residents by orchestrating meetings between city officials and representatives of neighborhood associations, and his administration introduced a series of environmental education programs.

Environmental education is critical in a country such as Brazil, where many of the citizens do not recognize the importance of protection of natural resources. This lack of public awareness can be a considerable barrier to implementing successful waste management policies. A 1998 poll conducted by the São Paulo-based Consumer Protection and Defense Foundation (PROCON—*Fundação de Proteção e Defesa do Consumidor*) revealed that only one out of seven city residents was doing any kind of recycling, and only 10% of those interviewed considered garbage separation as a "personal contribution towards a future solution for the trash problem."[22]

Under the outreach initiative, neighborhood associations in Curitiba met with city officials in the Fruet government on a weekly basis and discussed the environmental problems affecting residents in each district. Over time, Curitiba public officials transformed these gatherings into instructional sessions for the "systematic dissemination of information about the importance of environmental protection as [a] fundamental factor for improvements in [the] quality of life."[23] These environmental education programs eventually evolved into a required course in environmentalism in the city public schools.[24]

In 1985, for the first time in almost 20 years, Brazilians went to the polls to vote for mayors of the state capitals. Curitiba's citizens elected Roberto Requião, a well-known politician from the Brazilian Democratic Movement Party (PMDB—*Partido do Movimento Democrático Brasileiro*), the political group that for two decades opposed the military regime. The democratic transition coincided with the emergence of several social movements pressing for better living conditions, and Mayor Requião took charge in January 1986, promising a government that would rely on citizens' participation in public policy making. One of Requião's first initiatives was to sign legislation approved a few months earlier by the city council establishing the Municipal Department of Environmental Protection (*Secretaria Municipal do Meio Ambiente*). This new department evolved from the municipal division of parks and recreation, and its creation underscored the government's focus on environmental quality. The Municipal Department of Environmental Protection was charged with developing public policy on waste management, arborization and green area preservation, and ways to reduce degradation of the urban space. In the words of one public official, "we had an enormous concern, and were interested in curbing the criminality and offenses against the environment. To do that, it was necessary to have comprehensive laws in our municipality."[25] By 1991, Mayor Lerner signed into law *(Lei 7.833)* a city council bill that granted the department enforcement powers to inspect and combat "all socioeconomic activities that may harm the urban environment."[26]

By the late 1980s, Curitiba had become a pioneer in Brazil in the sector of waste management. Its recycling program, "Garbage that is Not Garbage" (*Lixo que não é Lixo*), was the first of its kind in a country where the majority of residential trash is left in precarious and filthy open sky landfills, the so-called *lixões*.[27] Through educational campaigns in the city public schools and community programs, residents were persuaded to separate solid and inorganic garbage—paper, glass, metal, and plastic—for later recycling. It is estimated that 70% of Curitiba's households are engaged in some kind of solid waste separation. Each month the municipal agency collects more than 2,000 tons of recyclable materials, 20% of which is processed for reuse at the Campo Magro recycling plant. Meanwhile, of the total trash produced by the city of São Paulo, only 1% is separated for recycling. In the city of Porto Alegre, capital of Rio Grande do Sul state, the proportion is 5%.[28] According to Jonas Rabinovitch, Curitiba citizens "recycle paper equivalent to nearly 1,200 trees each day." It is also estimated that Curitiba saves about US$60 million a year based on calculations that in Brazil for each ton of garbage that is recycled, it is possible to save US$435.[29]

Sergio Tocchio, former municipal secretary of environmental protection, has observed that an adequate garbage management program does not involve major complexities but it does require education. The secret, he once declared, was not to impose rules and not to overburden people but to show them a better way to do things. Education has been a key factor behind the success of initiatives to attack the solid-waste problem in Curitiba. In addition to being part of the curriculum in municipal schools, lessons in urban ecology have also been promoted by the local media through radio, TV, and newspapers ads such as the following example: "Please separate used paper, because in this way we can make new paper, saving many trees. Used metal becomes a new product, reducing mining activities. Do separate. Separate glass bottles and we will de-pollute the environment. What about transforming old plastics into new plastics? Garbage that is not garbage does not go to the garbage can."[30]

In the face of financial pressures that limited the number of garbage trucks the city could use, the Curitiba city hall came up with an innovative idea in 1989 called the "Garbage Purchase" (*Compra do Lixo*) program. Specifically designed for low-income families, mostly residing in peripheral neighborhoods, the program has helped to clean up sites that are difficult for the conventional waste management system to serve. Residents collect their own trash and deposit it in stationary municipal bins. Working together with the neighborhood associations, the government provides bus tickets for each filled garbage bag. The Garbage Purchase program also led to the creation in 1991 of the "Green Exchange" (*Câmbio Verde*), whereby residents exchange recyclable waste for a basket of vegetables. Over the years the Green Exchange program has become the centerpiece of Curitiba's government waste management policies. According to city hall, every month at least 20,000 people exchange about 400 tons of recyclable materials for 100 tons of vegetables. The exchange is made in 78 sites maintained by the municipal government in different districts. Curitiba's public officials laud the program for its far-reaching benefits: the city is cleaner, residents are becoming more informed about environmental issues, and low-income families benefit as they receive their bag of fresh produce. In addition, some 20,000 small agricultural producers in the rural areas surrounding Curitiba profit by having the municipal government as their main customer. The collected garbage ends up at the municipal recycling plant, where the more attractive and sought after materials are sold to private recycling firms. The government earmarks these proceeds to the *Fundação de Ação Social* (Social Action Foundation), a municipal agency that articulates and manages the city welfare policies.

Another successful municipal initiative linked to waste management in low-income areas is ECOS (the Environmental Program for Adolescents), formerly *PIA Ambiental*, in operation since 1990. In partnership with neighborhood associations, the government offers a series of activities for children between ages 4 and 12. In relatively small centers, which in many cases share space with the neighborhood association, participants are introduced to basic concepts of hygiene, health, and nutrition, and become familiar with the growth of plants in gardens and orchards. ECOS activities are integrated into the "Garbage Purchase" program, and children can exchange bags filled with solid waste for notebooks and other school materials. Since its inception, the program complements formal education programs, and participation does not require official enrollment. From the moment the center opens its doors in the morning with the arrival of a neighborhood association representative or a municipal employee, the children are welcomed in and can stay there until the afternoon. Currently, in its dozens of units located in different neighborhoods, the program receives an average of 5,000 children each day.

Environmental education in Curitiba was extended to the university level with the creation of Brazil's first open Environmental University (*Universidade Livre do Meio-Ambiente*) in 1991. Located in an impressive wooded area within the city limits, the university, also known as *Unilivre*, offers certificates in natural resources management at low tuition costs. It has attracted students from different parts of the country, especially government employees at the city level and some private sector executives. As impressive as it is, Unilivre may not be the most remarkable of the municipal educational initiatives developed by local authorities to enhance Curitiba's urban space. With far-reaching implications, *Faról do Saber*[31] (Lighthouse of Knowledge) is an innovative library system with 45 units located in different neighborhoods. It is designed to enhance residents' access to education, to improve the quality of public areas, to promote the city's cultural traditions, and to reduce crime. Inspired by the ancient Library of Alexandria, the *Faról do Saber* buildings are tower-shaped and contain, on average, 6,000 volumes. No Brazilian city has ever made a public investment on the scale and with the objectives of *Faról do Saber*, which by now provides free Internet access to all library users.

Curitiba's public officials do not feel that these initiatives are either highly ambitious or only viable in the city that they run. On the contrary, they stress that incremental initiatives toward environmental protection and public campaigns to promote them can succeed elsewhere as long as residents are involved in the process and can understand it and feel that they benefit from the programs. The underlying strategy has been to keep it simple and to start with the basics, with municipal programs that are economical and easy and quick to implement. Sergio Tocchio has described the thinking behind this approach as follows:

> We don't start things talking about the greenhouse effect. It is much easier to educate the population when we deal with local problems, with the people's daily problems. The projects that we have, the "Green Exchange," the "Garbage Purchase," "Garbage that is not Garbage," and the PIA, derived from the city needs; and all these projects have presented more or less good results in terms of environmental education. These projects are running. The garbage selection works, there is no secret here. What would be the secret? It is just a truck circulating on the streets, ringing a bell. Why other cities do not do the same? Because they have not been able to engage the population. We know, today, through statistics, that about 70% of Curitiba residents do separate garbage.[32]

CEMPRE,[33] a Brazilian nongovernmental organization and an authoritative source on recycling activities, has emphasized that for most municipal governments, budgetary considerations prevent the implementation of selective garbage collection because the process costs eight times more than conventional pickups. Yet the primacy of such financial concerns arguably reveals a lack of understanding of the environmental problems posed by solid waste and represents a shortsighted approach to waste management. Public investment in selective garbage collection can produce important economic returns to municipalities. In the case of Curitiba, for instance, recycling activities as a result of garbage separation has created, in a decade, about 20,000 new jobs. Other recycling benefits include a new source of revenue for municipal governments, resulting from the sale of recyclable materials to the private firms; a cleaner urban space and greater awareness of the importance of environmental protection.[34]

CONTINUOUS IMPROVEMENT: CURITIBA'S APPROACH TO INTEGRATIVE URBAN DEVELOPMENT

Recognized internationally for its simple, flexible, and affordable solutions, Curitiba's master plan has oriented city growth for four decades. Through its implementation, economic development has been catalyzed and the urban space has been enhanced. Under the plan, Curitiba's mass transportation policies and environmental management programs are intertwined and serve as pillars of the urban development process. The mass transit system, in constant expansion, has contributed to a reduction in commuting times and more comfortable bus trips. Government campaigns to encourage people to ride buses instead of driving their cars have helped reduce fuel consumption per vehicle to one of the lowest rates in Brazil, despite the fact that Curitiba enjoys one of the highest levels of motor vehicle ownership per capita.[35] The vast public works required to put the rapid bus system in operation also demanded a complete overhaul of the city downtown, which has rejuvenated its dynamism. It is now a flowered boulevard with a dozen blocks reserved for pedestrians, a change that has revived businesses—big and small—in the city center. Use of the single fare system, now in place in other Brazilian cities, is a Curitiba pioneering initiative and has been recognized nationally and internationally[36] as a social policy that grants more mobility to the urban poor. These policies have helped to create public appreciation for the ways in which mass transit integrates different parts of the urban space and enhances social connections through increased mobility.

With a sound planning instrument in hand, Curitiba municipal authorities inaugurated a new era in Brazil focusing on urban ecology. Ordinances were issued for the location of manufacturing plants, an ambitious urban parks program was started, and a comprehensive waste management system, till today one of the most consistent in the country, was launched. Through incremental steps, successive governments in Curitiba demonstrated that the regeneration of city conditions requires an integrated environmental strategy encompassing waste management, sanitation, street arborization, public gardens, and urban parks.[37] Solid waste recycling has environmental, public health, and economic implications. It contributes to natural resource conservation through the reutilization of a variety of materials and has reduced pollutants in the atmosphere. More efficient garbage collection in conjunction with recycling improves the cleanliness of public spaces and can help prevent the propagation of insect-transmitted diseases. Recycling programs in Curitiba have generated thousands of jobs that benefit low-income residents. The extensive arborization program, the creation of urban parks, and the enforcement of land management regulations have had important repercussions on city living. In Curitiba, these programs have not only prevented urban degradation but they have also enhanced the urban space. Leisure and recreational areas are plenty and open to all city residents, and green areas have reduced the flooding problem that had afflicted the city for decades.

Environmental education, both at school and community levels, and the engagement of residents in the implementation of environmental programs, have also been part of the continuous urban development process in the capital of Paraná. Government action in these areas has created a pro-environment mentality within the city. Through public campaigns, city governments have impressed on residents the importance of urban forests as an investment in the community's future. In one of Curitiba's most visited urban parks, the Bariguí, a digital board displays how many trees are being saved per minute, thanks to the city garbage recycling programs. Public opinion surveys[38] revealed that Curitiba residents strongly agree that (a) more trees should be planted; (b) trees contribute to the quality of urban life; and (c) more green areas should be preserved. Environmental preservation policies are integrated into the city's urban planning process on the basis of the idea that there are no isolated actions in the development of a city. Curitiba, as has been observed by numerous planning experts, embodies the principle of the unity of the ecosystem applied to the planning process.[39]

The vast majority of Brazilian cities lack a comparably coherent planning process. São Paulo is a case in point—its urban programs, including those aimed at environmental protection, are in general erratic as they lack an integrative framework in which several aspects of city living can be considered. Curitiba is a case from which lessons can be drawn for the study of municipal governments' capabilities in achieving policy goals and for how governance can be improved in a country otherwise characterized by ineffective governments. The only city in Brazil, and likely one of the very few in Latin America, that has been able to implement, adapt, and maintain an urban planning instrument for decades, Curitiba illustrates the potential of local governments to address urban afflictions in the developing world.

ENDNOTES

1. See Kirdar (1997, p. 231).
2. Among others, see Etienne and Zioni (1999) and Rabinovitch and Hoehn (1995).
3. See Rabinovitch and Hoehn (1995, p. 10).
4. See in the Appendix an abridged version of the original *Plano Diretor.*
5. See, for instance, Rabinovitch and Leitman (1996).
6. North (1990, pp. 5, 73).
7. Other cities in Latin America, including Quito and Bogotá, have introduced bus rapid transit systems, which are similar to Curitiba. The key feature is the establishment of a traffic-free lane along axial roads. The system is attractive because of its relatively low cost. An estimate indicates that the establishment of a bus rapid transit network costs about US$5 million per kilometer, only 20% of the cost of underground railways (Lapper, 2006).
8. Curitiba Urban Transport Program, Inter-American Development Bank (1995–2000).
9. In Amsterdam, there are 400 km of bicycle routes and a fleet of 600,000 bicycles.
10. Rabinovitch and Hoehn (1995, p. 8).
11. Satterthwaite (1997, p. 1668).
12. Habitat I, in Canada (1976); The Earth Summit (Brazil, 1992) and Habitat II (Turkey 1996).
13. See Brugmann (1996).
14. Jacobi (1997, pp. 386–387).
15. UNCHS (1999, p. 228).
16. It is estimated that today half of the United States is engaged in some kind of garbage recycling with clear benefits to the urban environment. For instance, in 1990 recycling diverted some 34 million tons of trash away from landfills, and by the end of the decade the number soared to 64 millions tons *(The Economist*, July 6, 2002, p. 32).
17. As cited in Kreimer Alcira, Menezes, Munashinghe, Parker and Preece (1993).
18. UNCHS (1999, p. 59).

19. Measurements of the city green spaces include privately owned
    wooded areas protected by fiscal incentives; municipal parks, public
    gardens, and about 6 million square meters of arborization along city
    streets (as cited in *Curitiba: The Ecological Revolution*). Regarding
    the amount of green areas per inhabitant, the figure varies according
    to distinct ways it is measured. In any case—either 50 or 20 square
    meters—the green space per capita in Curitiba is much higher than
    the Latin America's average (3.5 square meters in urban centers),
    and also above the 16 square meters recommended by international
    organizations.
20. See Oliveira (1996).
21. *A Folha de Londrina* newspaper.
22. According to an interview to the newspaper *O Estado de S.Paulo*,
    January 4, 1999.
23. See Trindade (1997, p. 104).
24. In Brazil, most of the public education (from elementary to high
    school) is a responsibility of the states. Yet, some city governments,
    like São Paulo and Curitiba, run municipal schools. Curitiba has one
    of Brazil's best-equipped public education municipal systems, where
    environmentalism is a required subject in all grades.
25. As cited in Trindade (1997, p. 93).
26. The Law 7.833 (1991) instituted the Curitiba Municipal Environ-
    mental Policy. Its promulgation represented the culmination of sev-
    eral efforts to create an institutional framework for environmental
    programs in the city capital. As a result of the democratization and
    the new 1988 national constitution, in many cities, the legislatures
    debated, voted, and approved new municipal constitutions reflecting
    the political democratic arrangements. In 1990 Curitiba city coun-
    cil approved the municipal constitution (*Lei Orgânica do Município*)
    requiring the establishment, as soon as possible, of an Environmental
    Defense Law. A year later, the mayor signed the legislation 7.833. See
    also Trindade (1997, p. 102).
27. According to data provided by IBGE, the federal census agency,
    about 75% of the garbage produced by Brazilians is thrown into open
    sky landfills and 0.7% is deposited in ponds, creeks, and swamps.
    Only 25% of trash receives a more adequate treatment. In more than
    50% of Brazilian municipalities, the garbage's final destinations are

improvised landfill sites called *lixão*, usually a vacant piece of land, an open sky place, where garbage is thrown, abandoned, without any treatment with serious environmental implications.
28. See Fadel (2001).
29. Rabinovitch and Leitman (1996, p. 32); see also Verano (1999).
30. As reported by Trindade (1997, p. 106).
31. With information provided by Hackenberg and Andreiko (2006).
32. Cited by Trindade (1997, p. 113).
33. CEMPRE: *Compromisso Empresarial para Reciclagem* (Entrepreneurial Commitment to Recycling).
34. Assunção (1999).
35. Friberg (2000, p. 155); Matsumoto (2002, p. 4); and Fickett, Gellings, and Lovins (1990).
36. See, for instance, Matsumoto (2002, p. 3).
37. Like in no other major city in Brazil, in Curitiba the appreciation for the trees is visible. Through public campaigns, city governments have tried to inculcate into residents the importance of urban vegetation. It has been emphasized that municipal tree programs are an investment in the community's future. In one of its most visited urban parks, the Barigui, a digital board displays how many trees are being saved by minute thanks to the city garbage recycling programs. Arborization projects in Curitiba have been the subject of a scientific survey to measure public attitudes toward urban trees, following the example of the United States where surveys of city trees have long been recognized as important for urban development purposes. Conducted by Araújo (1994), the survey reveals that Curitiba residents strongly agree that (a) more trees should be planted; (b) trees contribute to the quality of urban life; and (c) more green areas should be preserved. The Department of Environmental Protection (*Secretaria Municipal do Meio Ambiente*) is also in charge of other environmental concerns such as the management of both hospital and industrial waste, and the control of water, air, and audio and visual pollution.
38. See Araújo (1994).
39. Bongestabs (1983).

CHAPTER 3

EXPLAINING
INSTITUTIONAL CHANGE

The realization of the urban society calls for a planning oriented towards social needs, those of urban society. It necessitates a science of the city (of relations and correlations in urban life). Although necessary, these conditions are not sufficient. A social and political force capable of putting these means into oeuvres is equally indispensable.

—Henri Lefebvre[1]

The contrasts over the last four decades between the urban development process in Curitiba and those in other large cities in Brazil, particularly São Paulo, underscore the importance of the internal dynamics of governments. This factor goes a long way in accounting for the different responses local governments made to the similar challenges each faced in confronting population shifts, economic growth, industrialization, and national political-economic constraints. Given the fact that state intervention has been pervasive in Brazil, it is reasonable to assume that the failures and successes of urban policies must owe a great deal to how well city governments are able to govern. The governance strategies pursued in Curitiba and São Paulo are not distinct at the level of government action *per se*. Rather, São Paulo's record is not encouraging because, in general, city policies there have been misguided or misdirected. Over the four decades between 1965 and the first years of the 21st century, successive São Paulo governments have pursued either poorly conceived or inefficiently executed policies. In comparison, governments in Curitiba, in the same period, have demonstrated more capacity and ability to control city policy-making and have been able to generate more effective policies and take more coherent decisions in response to city growth.

The case of Curitiba has given rise to a "chicken or egg" debate in Brazil: does its government work better than others because the city is neat, tidy, and functional, or has Curitiba become a more livable place because it has had better government practices than other cities in the rest of the country? A closer look at the city's recent trajectory might help to resolve this conundrum. During my field interviews, several people recalled a time when the capital of the Paraná State was depressing, lackluster, and suffering from so much neglect that residents were afflicted by an inferiority complex. According to these respondents, people were skeptical about the city's ability to modernize its infrastructure, to develop a competitive economy, and to get first-class public services. Curitiba's downtown was in decay; public transportation was scarce and highly inefficient; floods were a major problem; and not even in their wildest dreams could Curitiba residents imagine that one day their city would attract foreign investment and international attention. Until the mid-1970s, Curitiba was not an urban center that attracted much attention even within its own state, lagging as it did behind Londrina, Paraná's second-largest city. The contrasting ways in which successive governments in both São Paulo and Curitiba dealt with the malaise brought about by uncontrolled urbanization are illustrative of how a public entrepreneurial approach to urban development can make a difference in terms of the quality of city growth and the likelihood that certain urban programs will or will not succeed.

In the mid-1960s, when the military came to power in Brazil, the country's patterns of development started to change drastically. Imbued with a nationalist ideology and having economic modernization as one of its major goals, the central government's main strategy was industrialization. Brazil's rulers sought to reduce the country's dependence on imports, especially capital goods and heavy machinery. Several state companies, the so-called *estatais*, were created to fulfill that objective, and at the same time new incentives were given to attract foreign direct investments. Increased mechanization of the agricultural sector led to a rural exodus of enormous proportions that by the early 1970s saw some 13 million people abandoning rural areas for the major metropolitan centers, especially the state capitals.[2]

No urban government at that time was prepared for such an influx of new residents. Large waves of internal migrants overwhelmed the cities' public services, setting the stage for a chaotic urbanization process to which the military in power paid little attention. The first National Development Plan (PND I), put in place by the central government in the late 1960s, did not establish a clear national urban policy. Typical of an authoritarian regime, Brazil's rulers invested themselves with great powers and became the main actors of the country's destiny. The federal structure of government was retained but operated under strict centralized control. The military regime appointed governors and the mayors in state capitals, and though these officials were given some leeway in terms of local policies, their main task (and the easiest way for them to retain power) was to impose public order in their respective jurisdictions. In practice, this meant following the military's dictates for ensuring a passive civil society without leftwing agitation, union activism, or any meaningful opposition voices.

The pressures of rapid urbanization in the 1960s helped convince city leaders in São Paulo and Curitiba that new urban master plans were needed. Both cities had urban plans that dated back to the 1940s, but in each case the plans had long become obsolete even before the challenges of industrialization and in-city migration came to be felt. Urban planners, architects, engineers, and economists drew master plans replete with proposals to deal with the environmental problems, housing shortages, and inadequate public transportation systems that each city was struggling with. Rather than treating the symptoms of the burgeoning urban crisis, these planning instruments were intended to be blue-prints for the future that would give city governments the tools they needed to shape the urban environment.

PUBLIC ENTREPRENEURS: POLITICAL COMMITMENT AND URBAN REFORM

The adoption of the 1965 master plan has proved to be a watershed for Curitiba. Through a process of incremental implementation, city governments revamped the urban space and enhanced the provision of public services to such a degree that Curitiba is now in a distinguished position within urban South America. Before the adoption of this innovative urban planning strategy, the capital of the Paraná state was a lackluster urban center, devoid of economic dynamism, and deprived of a reliable urban infrastructure. If it had been left to the whims of uncontrolled growth, as happened elsewhere in Brazil, Curitiba would likely have remained unorganized and still be struggling with serious transit and transportation problems. It might share the fate of many other cities in Brazil and Latin America, being stranded in a perpetual crisis born of the inability of city governments to commit themselves to urban enhancement and policy reform.

What is distinct and notable in the Curitiba case is that the public officials' commitment to urban reform generated an array of city policies that improved the 1965 master plan instead of derailing it. Especially important, this kind of governmental commitment also created a critical mass among city planners and residents alike that focused on continued improvements in urban living. Architects, engineers, economists, political scientists, journalists, and other professionals became involved in public debates and seminars designed to analyze city policies. The process engaged the citizenry and empowered them to press for change. Even though all of Curitiba's problems have not been solved, and new problems continue to arise as the city experiences one of the fastest growth rates in the country, a commitment to improving city policies has become a prerequisite for local government, which is a striking difference from the prevalent situation in Brazil. From the days of an alleged "inferiority complex," *Curitibanos* today enjoy one of Brazil's highest living standards and are beginning to take as "just normal" the visits of mayors from Latin America, the United States, and elsewhere, all of whom are interested in learning something about Curitiba's experiences with urban planning.[3]

As it occurred in São Paulo, Rio de Janeiro, Belo Horizonte, and Porto Alegre (the other major state capitals in the south-southeast corridor), Curitiba also experienced an earlier round of urban transformations in the first half of the 20th century. In 1941, Mayor Rozaldo Leitão hired the French architect Alfred Agache to revamp the city's landscape with the enhancement of streets and creation of boulevards. Agache arrived in Curitiba with sound urban planning credentials; among them, the fact that he had been in charge of the creation of Canberra, the Australian capital. He took 2 years to develop a new blueprint for Curitiba. The project was based on the tenets of modern urbanism expressed in the Athens Charter, according to which the city has to have certain functional characteristics.[4] Agache's idea was to divide Curitiba into particular sectors: a commercial center, an administrative unit, a university campus, a military compound, and several residential areas. In October 1943, Mayor Alexandre Beltrão received Agache's plan, which was to be only partially implemented because of an alleged lack of resources.[5] According to Curitiba-based historian and political scientist Dennison de Oliveira, however, the Agache plan quickly became outdated in the face of Curitiba's explosive growth.

Through the 1950s, the inability of Curitiba local governments to adopt or adapt Agache's proposals became highly detrimental to the city, which started to grow in a disorderly manner. In the early 1960s, the state government announced plans to intervene in the destiny of the state capital. At that time, Governor Ney Braga, a politician on good terms with the military group in power, developed an industrialization strategy for the state with its capital city as the focal point. The newly elected mayor, Ivo Arzua, based his electoral campaign on a platform centered on the need to shape Curitiba's urban growth. His proposals were formulated in large part with the input of young professionals who had just graduated from the newly created Architecture and Urban Studies program at the Federal University in Curitiba. Discussions concerning the need for city planning in Curitiba were also influenced by the foundation of Brasília, the country's new capital. Yet it soon became very clear to Curitiba's urban planners and politicians that while urban planning was a great idea, the Brasília model was not.[6]

One of Mayor Arzua's first initiatives was the establishment of a planning commission. Its main focus was on the need to implement a consistent land use policy to avoid chaotic growth. The commission developed a series of studies addressing a variety of urban problems such as the eradication of shantytowns, the creation of new train stations and the introduction of new bus lines. Thus, in the 1960s a conjunction of factors—the mayor's interest, the contribution of professionals and university-based debates about the city's future—triggered a completely new public discourse in Curitiba, which was focused on the benefits and disadvantages of urbanization, on how to address current problems and how to avoid future ones. The notion of how "to think the city" began to take hold in Curitiba.

The major constraint in going forward was the need to find funding for the proposed urban projects, as the state governor rejected the requests made by city hall. Financial resources would only be possible if the city government were able to present an integrated urban planning proposal tying together land use, economic development, and city infrastructure development. Arzua accepted the challenge and secured city government approval to hire a São Paulo-based architectural firm, Serete, *Sociedade de Estudos e Projetos*. As noted previously, Jorge Wilheim, who was also active in promoting urban development in São Paulo, was the architect in charge. Recalling these events more than 30 years later, Wilheim believes that the greatest difference in the planning processes in the two cities, and one that can explain the divergent outcomes realized, is that "the Curitiba plan did not remain in the drawer."[7]

The determination and commitment of Mayor Arzua were critical factors in the plan's later implementation as he mobilized much of city hall's human and material resources to ensure the design of a comprehensive blueprint to enhance the urban space. Facing city council opposition, the mayor offered local legislators certain guarantees that their approval would be required in matters of urban development. Above all, the mayor understood that potential obstacles could be more easily overcome if the proposals received widespread public support. Therefore, Arzua decided to open a public debate about urbanization and urban planning and invited architects, engineers, sociologists, economists, professors, and lawyers to city hall meetings to discuss the city's future. For several months the press covered the discussions. Through this educational/public relations campaign, the mayor was successful in getting city residents to embrace the master plan. A few years later, this popular support proved to be extremely helpful for the city government when it had to seek alliances to go ahead with urban development proposals in accordance with the master plan.

The original planning commission was later transformed into the Institute of Research and Urban Planning of Curitiba (IPPUC), whose mission was to oversee the new urban projects. Seen at its inception as just another municipal agency, the IPPUC proved to be essential in enabling subsequent governments to adhere to the city plan. In its 40 years of existence, the IPPUC has never departed from its major commitment to urban policy. This commitment made possible what had been virtually impossible for other city governments in the country: the transformation of a master plan into a dynamic policy instrument flexible enough to be adapted to meet the ongoing challenges of urban growth. Without the IPPUC's continual studies and proposals, it is very likely that the original Curitiba blueprint would have met the same fate as the plans designed for other cities, like São Paulo: they either remained in the drawer or their implementation failed due to ill-conceived projects or the inability or unwillingness of local public officials to make the plan work according to their city's dynamics. The IPPUC has thus contributed to the establishment of an institutional framework that favors urban development. The IPPUC's reputation, prestige, and image as a respectable government entity that develops innovative ideas for improvements in several aspects of city living—from transportation to recreational areas and housing projects—are by now so pervasive that no candidate to public office in Curitiba can hope to be elected without making a commitment to keep and enhance the urban development process.

Serete's original master plan focused on road infrastructure and key transportation projects. From this foundation and with the IPPUC's input, successive city governments have incrementally developed and implemented a comprehensive urban strategy. The evolving set of policies include land use regulations for building construction, arterial roads with dedicated bus lanes, a public transportation system that allows for constant expansion, extensive public works to combat floods, an urban park program that has made Curitiba one of the world's greenest cities, and several waste management projects including an innovative recycling initiative that both contributes to environmental protection and provides

Figure 1. Institutional framework.

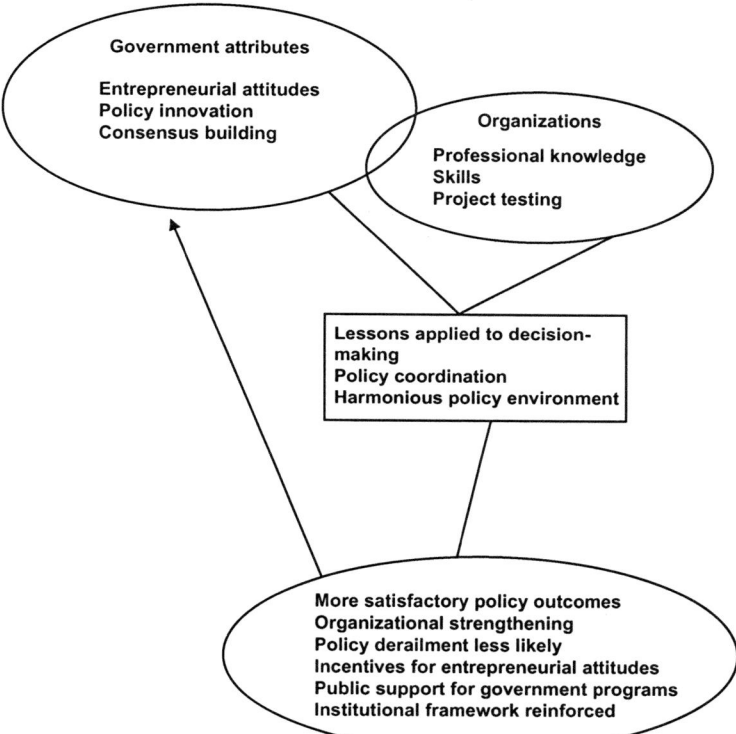

Note. Figure 1 schematizes the dynamics of an institutional framework more likely to lead to a successful governance strategy.

employment opportunities for the poorest segments of the population. Other aspects of the development strategy include creation of an exclusive area for factories and shops in the south of Curitiba, a pioneering university dedicated to environmental studies, low-income housing projects through self-building methods, and an extensive system of bicycle routes.

Curiously, some Brazilian thinkers, who recognize that the country has long been experiencing an urban crisis, do not see the concept of a master plan as an appropriate response for the urban decay, city mismanagement, and hardships endured by the population in the face of decrepit infrastructure and precarious public services. They regard the master plans conceived in Brazil as mere copies of models developed in the industrialized world and which are therefore not applicable to the Brazilian reality. Their argument stresses that urban planning projects are in fact instruments of domination used by elites to defend their own interests in the city, especially regarding land use and real estate speculation. These critics maintain that the upper classes and some intellectuals mystify the technical approach as having a "magical power to solve urban problems."[8] According to this argument, the advocacy of "scientific tools" and urban planning proposals as an apolitical response to urban problems represents a deliberate attempt on the part of the ruling class to disguise the fact that master plans are highly ideological.

Against this criticism, it must be conceded that because politics is a contest among different interests, many of the public policies that get put in place generally reflect the interests of those in power. The adoption and implementation of Curitiba's evolving master plan, beginning with Mayor Arzua's careful attention to building popular support for the proposals, has been and remains a highly political process. Yet this history of popular support and the continued evolution of the policy environment within Curitiba, to the point where no politician can reasonably seek office without pledging continued support of the planning process, belies the notion that Curitiba's master plan has been little more than a ruse for elite domination. *Curitibanos* have embraced the planning process for their city because of the improvements that have been made. Certain interests may have benefited more than others, but Curitiba has been successful in its urban strategy compared to the track record of other cities such as São Paulo.

Because Curitiba's urban planning model dates back as the longest in Brazil and has been evolving for almost four decades, it has become a fertile ground for critique. Whereas U.S.-based urban experts such as Alan Jacobs and Jonas Rabinovitch have praised the city government's approach toward "integrative urban programs,"[9] other critics, especially in Brazil, have pointed out what they called the elitist nature of the Curitiba urban planning process and observe that its policies have been implemented in a top-down fashion.[10] Although it is possible to argue that the evolution of Curitiba's urban development process has not been participatory, it should also be emphasized that it has not been authoritarian either. As noted previously, Arzua held numerous discussions of the master plan with neighborhood associations before its adoption by the city council. This was in addition to the seminars and workshops organized for architects, planners, and journalists. In the seminar "Colloque Sur L'Environment Urbain," that took place in Marseille, France, the urban expert Robert Joumard from the French Institute for Transportation stressed that one of the distinctive characteristics of Curitiba's urban policies is that governments "are being able to mobilize the citizenry, by engaging them in city projects."[11]

One of the features that make Curitiba's urban development process unique has been its adaptability. The solid institutional basis provided by the IPPUC enabled successive city governments to avoid being trapped by rigid master plans whose inflexibility works against their implementation. This adaptability, according to Wilheim, is the central characteristic of a master plan, because for him "a master plan is an action tool that evolves and is improved concomitantly to the development of the live organism we called city. For the same reason, the plan is not a rigid document. It is constituted by a planning body, by a basic document (the plan per se) which consists of maps and reports, and laws and regulations...The agency should have financial resources and autonomy, under city hall jurisdiction."[12]

How were Curitiba's city governments able to keep this commitment to urban planning? Why—and despite differences in political party affiliation—did the mayors opt for policy continuity, thereby avoiding the derailment that is so typical of Brazil's local governments? In contrast to the majority of the country's weak municipal agencies, which are subject to the vagaries of local politics and fraught with clientelism, how did the IPPUC become such a powerful urban planning policy tool? To answer these questions, we must take a closer look at the role that municipal agencies have played in Curitiba's urban planning process.

MUNICIPAL AGENCIES: A CATALYST FOR CHANGE

Previous studies of Curitiba's urban development process have singled out the critical role played by the IPPUC.[13]

In a country that lacks a planning tradition and where urbanization has taken place haphazardly and arbitrarily, the creation of this agency in the 1960s was a true innovation, and its evolution remains exceptional in the Brazilian urban experience. Unlike some city agencies that emerged with enthusiasm but withered and died out without notice, the IPPUC, four decades after its inception, continues to be a force behind the development process of the Paraná capital. Some skeptics in Brazil argue that a productive and sound municipal entity such as the IPPUC could survive only in a "unique" city like Curitiba. My counterargument is that to the degree Curitiba is qualitatively different from other Brazilian cities it is in large part because of the work of agencies such as the IPPUC. An array of specialists within the agency monitors the city's development and attempts to anticipate problems and develop solutions before they arise. The ideas generated by the IPPUC are taken to city hall and from there to the respective municipal departments where the plans are analyzed in terms of their applicability. This constant process of analysis and testing produces feedback that leads to improvements in the IPPUC's original ideas. Under these conditions, by the time the projects are begun, they address real problems and needs, and are more likely to produce positive outcomes. Curitiba's successes over the years appear to have less to do with the implementation of a particular technical planning model than with the accumulation of knowledge within the IPPUC. In addition to having skills according to their respective specializations, the agency's professionals also have a deep knowledge of the city. As a consequence, the IPPUC is in control of the urban space. The agency's input into the planning process is seen by the society as substantial and reliable, and governments risk ignoring the IPPUC's contributions at their peril.

The early principals at the IPPUC—Jaime Lerner, Lubomir Ficinsky Dunin, Franchette Rischbieter, and Luis Forte Netto—were convinced that in addition to new and modern infrastructure, Curitiba needed a comprehensive urban strategy that could integrate a new road system, public transportation, land use regulations, and resource management. Their vision of urban planning was influenced by studies on urban evolution conducted by the Economics and Humanism organization, which was founded in France in the late 1940s by the Catholic priest Louis Lebret.[14] At that time, social critics were already looking for a "third way" in an attempt to escape from the rigidities of the Cold War and its Manichean worldview. According to the Brazilian urban scholar Claudino Luiz Menezes, Lebret envisioned a movement that would put Protestants, Catholics, and communists together to remove the impediments to social development. As part of that vision, the way urban societies were organized was seen as one of these obstacles, and urban planning was considered an indispensable tool to eliminate those barriers.[15]

Lebret's main postulate concerned the need for action at all levels of community life, but with the proviso that it was imperative to understand first the reality of a given situation to take the proper action. As applied to the urban space, the Lebret doctrine expresses a deep belief in the power of planning but it does not embrace a single model of planning. Instead, a great variety of models should be considered, taking into account, in each case, the specific structures and particular needs that exist. During the 1950s, Father Lebret lectured in several Brazilian cities. His influence reached Curitiba and was apparent in studies produced by the Sagmacs, a state government workshop whose original objective was to analyze Paraná's territorial characteristics.[16] Yet the diagnostics generated by Sagmacs went well beyond the state's physical attributes and introduced social questions into analyses of the development process. Almir Fernandes, a Brazilian engineer who has followed the IPPUC's evolution, has said that one of the factors that enriched the multidisciplinary urban planning process in Curitiba was the work developed by a team of specialists at Sagmacs under the leadership of Father Lebret. According to Fernandes, Lebret's influence was felt on the ideological, methodological, and professional aspects of the planning process in Curitiba because many of his students later became members of the government.[17]

Probably the most important characteristic of the IPPUC is that it has managed to avoid falling into the trap of being a typical planning commission. Paul Davidoff has defined the latter as a "non-responsible vestigial institution." Although he was referring to planning agencies in US cities, his comments are probably more widely applicable. Davidoff argues that planning commissions fail to produce expected results because, as independent agencies working separately from local politics, they are never able to gain political support. According to Davidoff, "the commissions are not responsible directly to the electorate, and the electorate in turn is at best often indifferent to the planning commission."[18]

Although it has a considerable degree of autonomy to propose urban policy, the IPPUC works under the control of city hall and the city council, which ensures that programs are not adopted based on a strict technical perspective. David Farbman has ably discussed the shortcomings of the latter approach.[19] He has observed that a "physical bias" permeates the work of urban planners, and thus he emphasizes that:

> The physical bias is an attitude on the part of the planner, which leads him to conceive the principles and techniques of his profession as the key factors in determining the particular recommendations to be embodied in his plans...The physically biased planner plans on the assumption (conviction) that the physical problems of a city can be solved within the framework of physical desiderata: in other words, that physical problems can be adequately stated, solved and remedied according to the physical criteria and expertise. ...There is room, then, in the planning thinking for physical principles, i.e., theories of structural inter-relationships of the physical city; but this is only part of the story, for the structural impacts of the plan are only a part of the total impact. This total impact must be conceived as a web of physical, economic and social causes and effects.

In this sense, the IPPUC's scope is broader than that of a mere planning agency and instead has the characteristics of a comprehensive urban development authority. The IPPUC's structure, which includes the input of a variety of professionals—architects, economists, sociologists, engineers, public health, and housing specialists—has allowed the evolution of an integrated development process that combines public works, environmental management, and industrial and social policies. Unique in Brazil, where the tradition of planning is almost nonexistent, the IPPUC—in concept and practice—falls within the category of progressive planning, which many urban experts believe is more likely to produce better governance practices. For Davidoff,[20] for instance, progressive city planners "will be concerned with physical planning, economic planning, and social planning. An expanded scope reaching all matters of public concern will not only make planning a more effective administrative tool of local government, it will also bring planning practice closer to the issues of real concern to the citizens. A system of plural city planning probably has much greater chance of operational success when the focus is on live social and economic questions instead of rather esoteric issues relating to physical norms." Along a similar line of thought, Wilheim has observed, "under the general conditions of underdevelopment, urban problems and solutions cannot be analyzed in isolation from those conditions. For this reason, urbanism, as a tool to transform the reality, must have a fundamental objective: to make a contribution to the process of overcoming underdevelopment, by acting specifically on the urban structures in order to transform and to employ them."[21]

Genesis and Evolution of the IPPUC

The urban development legislation that authorized the 1965 master plan also formalized creation of the IPPUC.

Although not all of the master plan's recommendations were implemented in the first few years, the initial political commitment was critical in charting later developments. Mayor Arzua left office in 1966, soon after the legislation was enacted; his successor, Mayor Omar Sabbag, provided a single contribution that, in the end, ensured the plan's survival. Under his command, city hall equipped IPPUC with the needed human and material resources to make the urban development process a reality. During his administration, the IPPUC enhanced its capabilities by investing in professional training and organizing a database of relevant information from domestic and foreign sources. The institute was intensively devoted to research and project design, even without having the certainty that any given project would be implemented in the future. IPPUC's first president, the architect Luis Forte Netto, expressed his determination to make the institute "the ultimate city agency" with a raison d'être "to think the city." Working under a broad urban perspective, Forte Netto brought lawyers, librarians, and aerial-photo experts to the IPPUC. His idea was to develop know-how, or in his words, "to put together the expertise of people who were both familiar with the city hall dynamics and with the urban fabric."[22]

Although public officials had already given their support to IPPUC, the organization struggled in its early years with a major obstacle: within the municipal departments, suspicion toward the new city plan was running high and some directors were demonstrating a clear unwillingness to follow the IPPUC directives. Forte Netto realized that to be productive, the new agency would have to build a different kind of working relationship with all other city departments. With the city hall's green light, the IPPUC designed and put in place an educational campaign to train city bureaucrats and make them familiar with the proposed changes contained in the master plan. Under the presidency of Forte Netto, the IPPUC produced the first studies aimed at dealing with floods and protecting green spaces. The agency also developed a seminal municipal housing policy for Curitiba, the first of this kind in Brazil, thanks to the research and doctoral dissertation of one its officials, the architect Marlene Fernandes. At that time, the IPPUC also promoted the first public debate on what would later become one of the city's most acclaimed achievements: the new public transportation system. At the end of his term, in 1968, Forte Netto recommended another IPPUC architect, Jaime Lerner, to be his successor.

When Lerner assumed office as the new IPPUC president, the urban development plan still lacked any concrete measures for its implementation. Lerner, like many others inside the IPPUC, believed that urban reform in Curitiba should start with new road and transportation systems. The architect Eloy Kochanny, an expert on traffic and road circulation who has worked for the IPPUC since the early 1970s, remembers that transit conditions in Curitiba were a nightmare at the time. Commuters had to pass through downtown to reach any neighborhood within city limits. The IPPUC, Kochanny recalls, conceived a comprehensive and integrated set of remedies that included a new transit system, a comprehensive transport network, land use regulations, green areas' protection, and the urban parks program. According to him, the IPPUC soon became the "heart of the municipal administration."[23]

It took a couple of years, however, until the IPPUC was transformed into a key player in municipal matters. At the end of the Sabbag administration, the country was being ruled by a more oppressive dictatorship. In power since 1964, the military rulers, starting in 1968, issued several "Institutional Acts," which in practice meant the abandonment of the constitution and the temporary suppression of legislative powers.[24] The hard measures were the military's response to a wave of social unrest that began that year as protests were also proliferating elsewhere.[25] In the Brazilian state capitals, students, union leaders, professors, and journalists took to the streets to denounce the government's abuses, censorship, and the suppression of individual freedoms. The country even witnessed the emergence of armed urban groups, whose main feat was the kidnapping in 1969 of the US ambassador Charles Elbrick, to Brazil, who was released, unscathed, a few days later.[26] The misperception that Brazil was embarking on a leftwing revolution triggered an extensive crackdown by the military that led to uncountable imprisonments, incidents of torture, and executions. During this period, thousands of Brazilians left the country in exile. Sensing the need to exercise greater control over the large urban areas, where political opposition was stronger, the central government suspended elections in the state capitals for undetermined time. With the acquiescence of the military rulers, the governors appointed the state capital mayors, including Paulo Maluf in São Paulo and Jaime Lerner in Curitiba.

The only similarity between mayors Maluf and Lerner was the manner in which they ascended to the top government position in their respective cities. Otherwise, striking differences in managerial style, policy design, and engagement in city politics quickly became evident. About this time, the Brazilian press started to pay attention to the incremental transformations that were taking place in Curitiba. It was during Mayor Lerner's first term (1971–1974) that the urban development process in Paraná's capital began to really get under way. This period also marked the maturation of the IPPUC as a substantive city organization, capable of facilitating government action on urban reform. According to the historian and political scientist Dennison de Oliveira, Mayor Lerner was responsible for an authentic revolution in the field of urban planning as "the new mayor had been IPPUC president, former member of the planning commission that worked with Serete, and therefore, was totally identified with the plan implementation."[27] Influenced by the ideas of Father Lebret, Mayor Lerner, with the support of an empowered IPPUC, mobilized the government resources to implement urban policies whose main goal was to orient city growth toward a more harmonious development.[28]

In view of the urban planning instrument that had been approved years earlier by the city legislature, the mayor initiated the implementation of several projects to tackle urgent needs. Starting with the overhaul of the city public transportation system, the first Lerner administration also developed flood control policies and an innovative urban park program, invested in downtown renewal and laid the foundation for the creation of the Curitiba Industrial City (CIC), Brazil's first municipal initiative in the area of local economic development. In the beginning, the mayor's proposals were received with a certain degree of skepticism and even some opposition.[29] Yet as these policies started to show results, the idea of urban planning began to captivate Curitiba residents and the country as a whole. At the end of Lerner's first administration, the Curitiba experiment in urban development had attained such visibility that the Ministry of Interior decided to create a governmental commission to investigate the reasons for its successes. The Brazilian Institute of Architects considered Curitiba's administration as "ideal" and the Brazilian Institute of Municipal Administration (IBAM) also recognized its merits.

The IPPUC played a critical role in the physical and socioeconomic transformations that took place in Curitiba starting in the 1970s. The economist Euclides Rovani was hired by the IPPUC in 1974, and his main responsibility was to supervise the implementation of the new public transportation system, which started operations in September of that year. Authorized to hire experts in mass transit, Rovani created a team that produced innovative solutions in a public service that otherwise is still in shambles in many Latin American cities today. The IPPUC came up with the idea of exclusive bus lanes on the streets and created a bus schedule with regular routes at a time in Brazil when such a practice was unheard of. As a result of fieldwork in France under the IPPUC's auspices, the Brazilian public transportation specialist Carlos Ceneviva brought to Curitiba (and in fact to Brazil) the concept of a single daily fare, no matter how many trips a passenger might make. Specialists regard the single fare as a key component of a sound social policy through which governments can improve people's access to urban facilities. Enclosed bus stops were another novel innovation to the bus system. However, according to Rovani, the government's commitment was the most significant aspect of Curitiba's improvements in its mass transit system. He has stressed in *Memória da Curitiba Urbana* (1990) that while the Curitiba government was striving to put in place a reliable mode of locomotion congruent with the needs of city residents, "in the rest of the country nobody was scratching their heads, thinking about public transportation; nobody thought that the public sector could make this kind of intervention."

In the 1970s, the pioneering work developed by the IPPUC to control floods and reduce the number of risky areas in the Paraná's capital laid the foundation for federal legislation, known as the Leman Act, to regulate the establishment of human settlements to keep a preserved area of 15 meters along the banks of waterways. The engineer Nicolau Kluppel conducted the principal research on flood control for the IPPUC. He remembers that when he began his work there was no vision regarding the importance of preserving rivers and water reservoirs in Brazil. The prevalent mentality endorsed canalizing rivers to prevent inundations. Kluppel was in charge of a multidisciplinary team that included engineers, architects, and economists who developed an innovative strategy to combat floods: rivers would continue their course and would be allowed to rise in times of heavy rains and new land use regulations would be used to bar construction projects in areas subject to flooding.

Instead of expensive public works, including the construction of concrete levees along the city's rivers, land along the riverbanks would be protected and transformed into green areas, which would allow for water absorption. In effect, the flow of rainwater would be taken care by nature itself. "Urbanization is responsible for flooding and not the rivers," Kluppel declared in *Memória da Curitiba Urbana* (1992). According to him, it is easier and cheaper for governments to acquire land and transform it into parks and recreational spaces than to build expensive infrastructure to control floods, which seldom works. In 1975, the plan was transformed into a municipal law, and over the years, 25 critical areas in Curitiba were converted into municipal parks.

Another IPPUC official, the architect Luiz Masaru Hayakawa, oversaw the agency's first environmental management projects during the 1970s, long before a concern with being "green" became fashionable in the country. The initial project, during Lerner's first administration, used public funds to invest in arborization. A public campaign to plant trees along the city's streets quickly became popular with the vast majority of Curitiba's residents. In addition to changing the look of the city, the arborization project had a powerful impact on increasing environmental awareness. "Public education regarding environmental protection, garbage disposal and sanitation is the major lesson to be drawn from the Curitiba experience," says the architect Angel Walter Bernal, who in 1971 was the director of the Curitiba

Department of Recreation. In 1977, Bernal organized, in Curitiba, Brazil's first national conference on urban parks and gardens.

With support from the mayor, the IPPUC staff transformed the agency into a laboratory of ideas. Soon, it became known as the "Sorbonne of Juvevê," the city district where the institute was founded. Curitiba's urban policies have evolved incrementally with continued input from the IPPUC. Much of its original work remains in place and has served as the basis for expansion of the urban development process. The IPPUC's local prestige in Curitiba has expanded to national and international recognition. It has become an international center for training urban planners, and some of its members have been hired by city governments both in Brazil and abroad as consultants to urban development projects. Over the lengthy process of urban reform in the capital of Paraná, the IPPUC has been a catalytic agent in the institutionalization of an urban policy process that has been embraced by successive governments.

BUILDING CONSENSUS AROUND URBAN VISIONS

Anisio Brasileiro, author of a comprehensive 1999 study of Curitiba public transportation, identified the city public sector's ability to manage conflict as one of the factors behind the series of successful municipal public policies. The current consensus within Curitiba regarding urban development has its roots in the outreach by Mayor Arzua and his team of young planners who realized the importance of popular support in legitimizing the urban planning process. Brief mention has already been made of the yearlong series of workshops and seminars titled "Curitiba of Tomorrow" (*Curitiba de Amanhã*), and the numerous neighborhood meetings that helped launch the innovative planning project. Under the supervision of engineer Dúlcia Auríquio (who years later would serve as IPPUC president), the seminars disseminated documents and brochures to the populace at large that stressed, "the planner is not a god at all, conducting the mortals to unknown lands. ...The public interests must be found in the public, who ought to approve its own future."[30] During his meetings with community representatives, Mayor Arzua also tried to dispel the idea of planning as a bureaucratic and static process. In one of his public statements in 1965 he said, "urban planning is not a straitjacket. It must have a structure, but also several components that should evolve according to the socioeconomic conditions. Any rigid planning is wrong. As the needs and aspirations of people change, the national and international conditions that shape urban planning also change."[31] The media's extensive coverage of the seminars and discussions also helped build popular support for a new approach to urban development.

At the same time, the government initiated a far more complex strategy of negotiation with some specific nongovernmental actors whose support was considered important. Bus company owners, construction firms, the local chamber of commerce, and Paraná's industrialists became city hall's main targets as public officials contemplated profound transformations in the public transportation system, downtown renewal, and strict land use regulations. This inclusionary approach is an example of what Paul Peterson identified in *City Limits* as "consensual politics," where conflicts within the city tend to be minimal, "and local support is broad and continuous," not because of the absence of disagreements but mainly because the principal actors share a preference for accommodation.[32]

Mass transit in Curitiba always has been run by private enterprises. Both Mayor Arzua, who obtained formal approval for the city plan, and Mayor Lerner, who implemented the proposals, never sought to transfer control of the bus system to the municipal government—unlike efforts to do so in other state capitals, São Paulo among them. Instead, Arzua and Lerner understood that to revamp mass transit operations, the better option would be to reach out to the business class and offer some incentives to the private sector. City hall engaged the bus company owners by assuring them that they would face minimal competition–such as from private cars and the taxicabs— because no other public mode of locomotion would be allowed in Curitiba.

Anisio Brasileiro has emphasized this unique character of Curitiba and its surrounding localities within the metropolitan area where there are no small vehicles (vans and microbuses) competing in the transport of passengers. In other Brazilian and Latin American cities, such as Porto Alegre, São Paulo, and Lima, this modality of public transport—sometimes called informal—has proliferated, almost without government regulation. However, in Curitiba, the local government has inhibited the presence of alternative modes, thus assuring a permanent market for the bus companies. With this strategy, local authorities secured the participation of a significant private partner in the urban development model. From its beginning until today, public transportation policies in Curitiba have always taken into account the necessity of avoiding major confrontations with the bus company owners. Although it is true that the strong public sector intervention has eliminated competition, thus creating a sort of private monopoly in the city transport sector, the positive aspect of the story is the system itself, which, says Brasileiro, has "unquestionable merits...and is highly valued by the commuters." The relatively high degree of public satisfaction is also due to the fact that bus companies make constant investments to improve the system. They are aided in these efforts by strong public sector oversight and the relentless pursuit of technological innovation through research conducted by IPPUC. The innovations introduced in Curitiba—express bus lanes, biarticulated buses that can move 20,000 people per hour, enclosed bus stops, transfer terminals, and a single fare—are, according to Brasileiro, "pioneering measures in the world context" that would not be possible without a public-private partnership.[33]

In addition to the relationship with the bus companies, governments in Curitiba have also pursued consensual politics by seeking agreements with other private actors who might be affected by, or whose actions might influence, the urban development process. There is no concrete evidence to suggest formal participation of the local business class and other nongovernmental actors in the government's decision-making process. Yet it is possible to demonstrate several instances in which governments in Curitiba have taken into account the private sector's interests as a way to avoid the derailment of urban reform.

The beginning of a working relationship between Curitiba's public and private sectors took place in 1965 with the celebration of a seminal conference on industrial development in Paraná's capital. Organized by two powerful business groups—the Federation of the Industries of the State of Paraná (FIEP—*Federação das Indústrias do Estado do Paraná*) and the Paraná Chamber of Commerce (ACP—*Associação Comercial do Paraná*), the seminar brought together the city's economic elite and the highest-ranking public officials to discuss strategies to bring industrial investments to the area. As emphasized in the conference's final document, the participants agreed that the formulation of an aggressive policy to accelerate socioeconomic development in the region should be the highest priority.

By 1971, the relationship between the local government and the business class was further solidified through the First Conference on Curitiba Economic Development, organized by city hall and the ACP. Taking as its starting point the discussions held at the previous 1965 seminar, the new workshop focused on what a few years later would radically transform Curitiba's economic basis: the creation of the Curitiba Industrial City (CIC). This initiative is considered a watershed in the city's history, as it was instrumental in making Curitiba one of the country's most attractive locations for multinational investment.[34] At a time—the early 1970s—when the military government had an ambitious national industrialization plan, Curitiba's economic elites felt that they needed to be part of the process. In a 1971 document, the ACP stressed that "the development has to be organized, stimulated and sought. We cannot expect that development will come naturally, especially in this special Brazilian moment in which several regions are almost waging a daily struggle to attract private and public investments."[35]

Curitiba's business class realized that a close relationship with local authorities was needed for them to participate in the national industrialization plans. The local elite was aware that to be eligible for federal credits and to seek partnerships with foreign companies, the city would need to demonstrate that it was capable of undertaking the major public works' projects needed to develop its physical infrastructure and expand the road system. The city created the Curitiba Council for Financial Policies, whose goal was to advise the mayor on ways to attract domestic and foreign capital investment. The Council was composed of the mayor, the president of the IPPUC, the ACP president, and representatives of several business sectors.

After prolonged negotiations, the CIC initiative became part of the city's urban strategy, under the regulations established by the 1965 master plan. With input from both the IPPUC and URBS, city hall took responsibility for all urbanization programs within the industrial city. The extensive project was the first local economic development initiative in Brazil to be managed by a municipal government. Lots considered of strategic interest were demarcated and later sold by the municipality to companies that were building factories in the industrial city. The local authorities also imposed new environmental regulations on the industrial area: within its 40 square kilometers, industrial units were not allowed to cut down any trees and all factories were required to have sewage treatment systems and equipment to measure effluent levels. The government set aside a vast tract of land surrounding the CIC where years later a major low-income housing project with 60,000 residential units was built. Multinational companies, among them Bosch, New Holland, Phillip Morris, and Volvo, were the first to submit applications to build factories in the industrial city, which later attracted hundreds of new companies. Some analyses of the CIC's impact on Curitiba's urban development process[36] indicate that a substantial number of companies transferred operations to the new industrial corridor; among them, the coveted capital goods factories As a result the profile of the local urban economy was altered with a steady growth of the city GDP as demonstrated in Table 6.

Following the approach that led to the establishment of the industrial city in the 1970s, the municipal government, in the early 1990s, took another step to promote economic growth with the creation of the *Barracões Empresariais* (Entrepreneurial Sheds), which work as small business incubators, operating with government support. Throughout the city, 12 incubators host more than 100 small firms, both in the manufacturing and service sectors, which have contributed to job creation and income generation, and have also been the places for worker training and skills acquisition. The incubators—similar to the industrial city—were not conceived in isolation. Rather, they form an integral component of the comprehensive urban strategy that has

Table 6. Gross domestic product 1985–2003 in Curitiba,
Paraná State, and Brazil—selected years.

Year	GDP (US$ Billions)		
	Curitiba	Paraná	Brazil
1985	3.53	20.20	310.90
1990	5.91	26.30	445.90
1991	5.43	23.20	386.20
1992	5.42	22.80	374.30
1993	6.45	27.10	430.30
1994	8.73	36.50	561.30
1995	10.56	44.50	718.50
1996	11.56	48.70	775.40
1997	12.10	50.07	804.10
2003	7.81	49.10	773.60

Source. IPPUC and Curitiba S/A.

been the landmark of Curitiba: established in previously
rundown areas, the incubators are at the same time induc-
tors of economic and of urban development. They have
the ability to regenerate the public space, thanks to the
emergence of new economic activities, the arrival of mass
transportation, and other public services, such as garbage
collection, in the localities where the incubators operate.

COPING WITH DISCORD

However, the local government's urban development proposals faced a series of challenges in the 1970s from the
powerful real estate sector, principally from the Association of Real Estate Managers (ADEMI—*Associação dos*

Dirigentes das Empresas do Mercado Imobiliário); the Trade Union for Acquisition, Sale and Lease of Properties (SECOVI—*Sindicato das Empresas de Compra, Venda e Locação de Imóveis*), and the Construction Industry Trade Union (SINDUSCON—*Sindicato da Indústria da Construção*). In a country where the land market displays speculative and exploitative characteristics, it is not hard to imagine the private sector's strong negative reaction to proposals of government intervention in the real estate market. Yet, following the 1965 master plan guidelines, Curitiba city hall would have to impose land use regulations, in the pursuit of a more harmonious development, and declare off-limits large amounts of urban area for sanitation, environmental, and recreational purposes.

In a public statement about the complexities of land use regulations in Curitiba and how they initially soured public–private relations, Mayor Samuel Ruiz (1975–1979) observed: "We did control city growth, but with incredible headaches, because we restricted the construction rights. The real estate sector declared war on us, against our team; there were numerous lawsuits, something crazy, but we endured."[37]

Obviously the real estate sector is interested in attractive urban areas in which investments—in commercial or residential units—will provide fast and substantial returns. Owing to the existence of land use regulations, construction projects in Curitiba have to follow strict guidelines in terms of localization and size of buildings. These limitations have produced clashes between building companies and city hall, whose control of construction permits and commercial licenses has been at the core of the public–private sector disputes. Whereas this type of conflict has never been completely settled, city governments have been able to manage the process and ensure the continuity of the urban development strategy. Retaining the preference for consensual politics rather than open confrontation, Curitiba's governments have kept a more or less permanent line of communication open with the real estate sector through regular meetings between business representatives and IPPUC officials.

Negotiations have sometimes led city hall to concede in the face of pressures from the private sector. For instance, there have been cases of undue concession of licenses and permits; and some city hall-approved proposals regarding building projects and land occupation have been rejected by the local legislature as a result of pressures coming from a powerful construction sector lobby.[38] Yet local public officials have also been able sometimes to turn the negotiations in their favor, as occurred with the approval of municipal legislation L.7841, which maximizes the use of land lots by authorizing the construction of new floors over existing buildings. The so-called *Lei do Solo Criado* (roughly, Law of Created Soil) is a common feature in several Brazilian cities. Specifically, it gives to city authorities the power to sell building rights to developers and property owners who add floors to a given building.[39] In Curitiba, the local government in 1991 managed to give some social character to the legislation by establishing that construction firms that enjoy the financial benefits provided by the enlargement of existing buildings have to transfer to city hall a percentage of value added to the property. The resources go directly to the Municipal Housing Fund (FMH), which supports low-income housing projects.

Curitiba's local authorities have gone to great lengths to ensure the success of urban reform. Although partnerships, consultations and negotiations with local nongovernmental actors partially explain how successive city administrations have been able to successfully implement urban development plans, intergovernmental relations have also played a role in the equation. The economist Alberto Maia da Rocha Paranhos, a former IPPUC official, says that despite federal government attempts in the mid-1970s to establish a working relationship with governments in São Paulo and Rio de Janeiro, only the Curitiba city hall was able to build a productive dialogue with the CNDU (*Conselho Nacional de Desenvolvimento Urbano*), the National Council of Urban Development. During the period of authoritarian rule, the military pursued certain urban development projects, not out of a concern with improving the quality of life, but mainly as a way to exercise territorial control and ensure public order. Curitiba's local officials took advantage of the opportunity this presented to get federal support to implement city plans.[40]

According to Paranhos, Curitiba city hall, with input from the IPPUC, benefited from this close relationship with the federal government, while the initial CNDU contacts with São Paulo and Rio de Janeiro came to naught because governments in those cities had nothing to offer in terms of a sound urban analysis.[41] Luiz Forte Netto, former IPPUC president, has observed that as a result of this intergovernmental dialogue and exchange of urban studies, the central government allocated considerable resources for Curitiba's urban development plans in the 1970s. In *Memória da Curitiba Urbana* he recalled that it was easy for city hall to obtain funds for several projects. Federal funds helped Mayor Jaime Lerner to institute a new road system with a structural roads network and create the industrial city, among other programs.

In the late 1970s, during the administration of Mayor Ruiz, the Ministry of Interior provided extra financial support to an innovative housing program developed by the Curitiba housing authority (COHAB), which introduced, for the first time in Brazil, a self-help building project. Eligible families obtained subsidized loans to acquire a small lot and building materials and start construction according to guidelines provided by city hall specialists. Although it is not a sufficient solution for the chronic housing shortage nationwide, the self-help building program was an alternative for thousands of families who lived in shantytowns. The government of São Paulo adopted the idea in the late 1980s.[42]

After a couple of years in San Francisco as a visiting professor of urban affairs at the University of California-Berkeley, Jaime Lerner was appointed mayor for the second time (1979–1983). He arrived at city hall just as social problems were mounting across the country in the face of a major economic crisis propelled by prohibitive fuel prices and the end of the Brazilian "economic miracle." Lerner was committed to the notion that urban development should have a positive social impact. Accordingly, he followed the previous administration's efforts to improve housing conditions by introducing the CURA project for the recuperation of urban communities.[43] This initiative initially focused on two city neighborhoods—Vila Isabel and Jardim das Américas. The CURA program provided street paving, established sewage connections, and built recreational areas to integrate these isolated communities with the rest of the city. In addition, Lerner enhanced the public transportation system with the introduction of the single fare, and designed a new model of action in municipal public health, with the creation of 12 community clinics focused on preventive care. At the end of his second administration, Lerner abandoned the military-supported political party and became a member of the left-leaning Labor Democratic Party (PDT—*Partido Democrático Trabalhista*). The national leader of the PDT was Leonel Brizola, a charismatic politician who, as a state governor in the 1960s, tried to lead a popular revolt against the military coup. Brizola went into exile, returning to Brazil in the late 1970s.[44]

After the darkest years of the military dictatorship passed, the tradition of consensual politics in Curitiba deepened with the presence of new actors in the public space. After 15 years of dominance, the military-backed Alliance for National Renewal (ARENA) started to lose ground. In the early 1980s, a new era of local politics was inaugurated in many state capitals, Curitiba and São Paulo among them, with the designation of mayors from the opposition party, the Brazilian Democratic Movement (MDB). In Curitiba, Mayor Maurício Fruet took office with the city undergoing major changes in response to a seemingly unstoppable migration from the rural areas. Social movements were blossoming throughout the country, increasing pressures on governments for democratization and better living conditions. Fruet continued the urban development program from previous administrations but wanted to make it more participative. The architect Omar Akel, a long-time IPPUC official, remembers that during the Fruet years, the IPPUC president, Rafael Dely, made participation a type of mantra in his administration. According to Akel, Dely opened the IPPUC to the community by creating new channels of communication with journalists, artists and social activists.[45]

During the three years of his administration, Fruet pursued this objective of making government more participatory. He convened dozens of public hearings to promote discussions on city issues among different groups in society, and he made countless visits to Curitiba's neighborhoods to understand the residents' needs and demands. Fruet also instructed his cabinet to be available and open to the population's claims and complaints. As part of his efforts to improve the quality of urban life, Fruet launched what was at the time a unique municipal initiative: he promoted environmental awareness through public campaigns and sought the support of neighborhood associations to implement new garbage disposal programs.

In 1985, Fruet's successor, Roberto Requião, became the first elected mayor after 20 years of military rule. In the complex web of power relations that characterizes local politics in Brazil, Requião and Lerner are archenemies. This enmity is driven less by ideological reasons and more by disputes over political power and control of resources in Paraná, Brazil's largest agricultural producer and the site of the country's largest source of hydroelectricity. Paraná has become an increasingly attractive place for foreign investments and possesses a much regarded modern and efficient port, the Paranaguá, which is a major outlet for Brazilian exports.[46] Despite his personal rivalries with Lerner and his distance from city public officials of the so-called "Lerner School" or "Lerner Group" (especially those inside the IPPUC), Requião assumed office without posing a major challenge to the urban development process that had started almost 20 years earlier. In the 1980s, the pursuit of quality of life was already ingrained in the public discourse in Curitiba to the point that the new mayor could not afford and justify derailing what had already been done.

Known as a man of social concerns, Mayor Requião focused his administration on improving health care. During his term, Curitiba pioneered the introduction of the country's first public health municipal system. Until then in Curitiba and in the majority of state capitals, public health assistance was a state government concern supported by state and federal resources. Mayor Requião decided to put city hall in charge of health care programs by creating 60 municipal clinics that operated around the clock. The medical profession opposed the new initiative at the outset, especially because nurses were put in charge of the clinics for practical reasons. The Curitiba Medicine Council, the physicians' corporative body, protested this decision, and some doctors abandoned their posts in the municipal health centers. Yet, in the end, Requião's ability to get the support of the local press for his main project guaranteed its success.[47]

The year 1988 marked the beginning of a new political era in Brazil with the promulgation of a democratic constitution, a legal instrument destined to revamp state-society relations. In that same year, municipal elections brought some hope for the afflicted São Paulo, with the mayoral election of Luíza Erundina de Sousa, a member of the Workers' Party (PT). Erundina's election represented a clear rupture with the conservative forces that had been in charge of the country's largest city for so many years. The expectation was that a mayor identified more with the populace would make better progress in dealing with the city's problems, but to do this, urban reform efforts would have to start from scratch. Meanwhile, in Curitiba, Jaime Lerner obtained an impressive majority, comfortably reaching city hall for a third time. In his inaugural speech in January 1989, there was no hint of a rupture with past administrations but just an outline of actions that would reinforce the city's achievements. Lerner, once more, emphasized the notion of consensual politics by proposing a partnership with the future, asserting: "we will seek partnership with everybody, by joining the living forces of the city, in order to establish, again, a reservoir of work and ideas."[48]

As mentioned in previous works,[49] the Curitiba governments' preference for consensus rather than confrontation has avoided the derailment of public policies and facilitated a continuity of governmental action. Although it is perhaps accurate to concede that the successes in urban reform in Curitiba are part of a larger project by local elites to modernize the region's economy and enhance its position in the international economy, nonetheless in addition to its alliances with local business groups, governments in Curitiba have also obtained the support of other society groups by associating urban programs with better living conditions. The latter has been emphasized by Dennison de Oliveira, for instance, when he said that "by allowing several trips with a single fare, the public transportation system provides to the workers an unlimited access to a public service that is one of the main domestic expenses. It is the same thing with the municipal program that exchanges recyclable waste for a bag of vegetables. In this way, the public sector not only saves some resources in garbage collection, but, mainly, it is allowing that ample segments of the low-income population feel as participants of a common project for the city."[50]

The broad and durable consensus has been beneficial both to the city and its governments. In an analysis of public policy outcomes in Curitiba over six administrations, from Lerner in 1971 to Lerner in 1991, Paul Hawken observed that all mayors have followed compatible policies and advanced prior achievements, thus generating a flow of interconnected, interactive, and evolving solutions. These ideas and responses to urban problems have been devised and implemented by partnerships among private firms, nongovernmental organizations, municipal agencies, community groups, neighborhood associations, and individual citizens. Hawken goes further by saying Curitiba is not a top-down, mayor-dominated city because of its record in encouraging entrepreneurial solutions.[51]

For reasons probably related to ideology or political preferences, those who are reluctant to give credit to or recognize the merits of Curitiba's urban development process argue that the master plan is essentially a piece of work developed by conservative governments. It should be mentioned, however, that it has only been during the two leftist São Paulo municipal administrations—those of Mayor Luíza Erundina de Sousa and Mayor Marta Suplicy—that some of Curitiba's initiatives have been adopted in São Paulo, among them the self-help housing programs, projects for downtown renewal and proposals to create green areas, and a series of urban ponds (*piscinões*) to control flooding.

Several urban planning professionals, among them Jorge Wilheim and Cândido Malta Campos Filho, agree that São Paulo residents are paying a high price for their city's chronic lack of direction. They argue that a successful urban development plan is far from being a technocratic instrument and that by encompassing plausible and sensible guidelines for transportation, car circulation, local economic development and land use regulations, its implementation can improve the quality of urban life for all residents. In 2000, the popular newsweekly *Veja* summarized the hardships for São Paulo by stating that:

> Without an updated and comprehensive vision, the tendency for city hall is to think in small terms, looking for localized solutions that generated new problems. A good master plan (*plano diretor*) reduces the possibility of fraudulent deals, as it is the case of some city councilmen (*vereadores*) who believe they own the city and can sell it in pieces. In addition to some technical components, the master plan requires a political

agreement. The city should elect a mayor that is able to think big and with a long term vision, and also willing to negotiate with all society groups.

Yet the politics of consensus, which has been a trademark of Curitiba's government for almost 40 years, has been practically absent in São Paulo.

ENDNOTES

1. "Theses on the city, the urban and planning," in *Writings on cities* (1996, p. 178).
2. Menezes (1996).
3. In 1999 the mayor of Los Angeles, Richard Riordan, visited Curitiba on a trip to South America with the single objective to find a solution for the dire public transportation problems in California's largest city. During contacts with Curitiba City Hall, Riordan expressed his government's intention to adapt the Curitiba transportation system in Los Angeles where the metro project had resulted in a major fiasco. In addition to its efficiency, the Curitiba bus system caught the attention of the Californian mayor because of its low cost: whereas in Los Angeles the construction of a subway mile was calculated in US$ 300 million, the cost of a bus system similar to Curitiba's is estimated at US$ 2.5 million per mile. Different from the subway in several aspects, Curitiba's bus network does not require expropriations, allowing the city government to save millions in payments to housing and business owners. Buses circulate on existing streets, on exclusive lanes created on the surface of arterial roads. There are several main express routes, which are integrated with other lines running to more distant neighborhoods. Riordan's presence in Curitiba was only one among more than a hundred foreign governmental delegations visiting the city each year. Interested in new urban planning experiences, some governments have applied some of Curitiba's innovations to their cities, as is the case of Cape Town, in South Africa. By the suggestion of the Inter-American Development Bank, the mayor of Managua, Roberto Cedeño, spent several days in Curitiba to learn how government action can alleviate urban problems in the Nicaraguan capital, a city, he said: "where quality of life is a very remote idea to us." Cedeño explained that a pressing problem in Managua was lack of public transportation, observing that some projects developed in Curitiba could work in his city. The approval of new IDB loans for urban infrastructure in Managua was dependent on a mayor's report assessing how some of Curitiba's projects could be adapted to Nicaragua's capital.

4. The Athens Charter refers to the document that emerged from the International Congress of Modern Architecture held in the Greek capital in 1933. The manifesto defines the objectives of city planning in terms of four functions: housing, work, recreation, and traffic. The Athens Charter's most celebrated supporter was the French architect Charles Le Corbusier. Brasília's design was based on the ideas coming from the Athens Congress.

5. *Gazeta do Povo,* April 30, 1996.

6. At the time of its foundation in 1960, Brasília embodied the dreams of both modernity in a country in the process of industrialization, and of a more egalitarian society. Conceived by the Brazilian architects Oscar Niemeyer and Lucio Costa, the new nation's capital was planned with the notion that a new urban space could be also an instrument of social change in the context of national development. In his insightful critique of the Brazilian capital, Holston (1989) observers that the rationale for the construction of Brasília was that it should be a model of different social practices, and that it would be an exemplar of progress for the rest of the nation. Both architects saw a modernist architecture and city planning as agents of change. Brasília was conceived not only to take development and progress to Brazil's heartland (which in part it did), but also to transform the class structure of the Brazilian society, by breaking with the traditionalism, stratification, and inequalities of the country's urban life. Holston analyzes how the city's evolution subverted its founding promises. He observes that Brasília's residents in fact reinforced the cultural values and social structures that the planners intended to destroy. Followers of the French architect Charles Le Corbusier, Niemeyer, and Costa planned a functional city with collective residential areas, the so-called *superquadras* (super-blocks) without room for slums. It is a city where pedestrian walk was never taken into consideration by the master plan. Very soon, the newcomers realized that they would need a car to live and work in Brasília. Today, public transportation in the nation's capital is precarious, shantytowns (*favelas*) surround the federal district, and it is believed that it is today Brazil's most segregated city. Brasília's construction started in 1957 by initiative of President Juscelino Kubitschek.

7. During an interview in his São Paulo office, May 2000.

120 URBAN BRAZIL

8. Villaça (1995, p. 47).
9. Alan Jacobs, faculty member at the University of California; former planning director for San Francisco and a prominent analyst of the Curitiba urban planning process. See, for instance, MacMargolis (1992, pp. 4250). Jonas Rabinovitch is the United Nations Senior Urban Development Advisor and lived for several years in Curitiba. He has written extensively about the evolution of the urban planning process in that city. See, for instance, Kirdar (1997).
10. See, for instance, Villaça (1995) and Garcia (1997).
11. In *Diário Popular*, April 16, 1995.
12. Wilheim (1965, pp. 123–124).
13. For instance, "Curitiba ecocity: Personal reflections on the most livable city in South America," by *Development Bank of Japan*; "Efficient transportation for successful urban planning in Curitiba," in *Solutions case studies*; Rabinovitch and Hoehn (1995); and Oikawa (1993).
14. Louis Joseph Lebret (1897–1966), French Dominican. Founder of the Paris-based *Economie et Humanisme* research center, which supported several similar organizations throughout the world. He was one of those who introduced the concern for global development within the Catholic Church, at the personal and social level. According to Vatican documents, Father Lebret was the main source of inspiration for the 1967 papal encyclical *Populorum Progressio* (On the Development of Peoples).
15. Menezes (1996, p. 73).
16. Literally: Society of Graphic and Mechano-Graphic Analyses Applied to Social Systems. Heavily influenced by Lebret ideas, the Sagmacs, in the 1960s, emerged in several Brazilian cities, São Paulo included, aiming to provide orientation for future master plans. Only in Curitiba were the Sagmacs proposals transformed into governmental action.
17. Fernandes (1990, p. 72).
18. Davidoff (1996, p. 314).
19. *A Description, analysis and critique of the master plan*, University of Pennsylvania (1959–1960, pp. 22–26), as cited in Davidoff (1996).
20. Davidoff (1996, p. 318).
21. Wilheim (1969, p. 89).

22. In *Memória da Curitiba Urbana* (1991, p. 65).
23. In *Memória da Curitiba Urbana* (1991, p. 272).
24. Later, the Congress was able to restart sessions, but restricted to two parties only: the pro-military ARENA (Alliance for National Renewal) and the MDB (Brazilian Democratic Movement). The democratic transition started in 1985.
25. For instance, Paris in May 1968, when university students staged dozens of demonstrations demanding freedom of speech and of movement. The major workers' unions adhered to the protests, calling for a general strike that practically paralyzed France. The unrest forced the government to hold a referendum that culminated with the departure from power of President Charles de Gaulle. There was also Mexico City, October 1968, with the so-called "Night of Tlatelolco," when hundreds of demonstrators were rounded up by plain-clothed state security agents during protests that took place in the Tlatelolco Square on the eve of the inauguration of the Olympic Games to denounce the government's attempts to suppress university autonomy. The precise number of deaths is still unknown; in the subsequent days, several opponents were detained by Mexican authorities. According to Mexican political analysts, popular support for the official Revolutionary Institutional Party (PRI) declined after the incident. A Brazilian journalist, Zuenir Ventura, authored an excellent narrative of the events in Brazil, *1968: O Ano Que Não Terminou* (Ventura, 1993).
26. Years later, after imprisonment and exile, the Brazilian journalist Fernando Gabeira, who commanded the kidnapping operation, narrated the event and delivered a critique of intellectual left in the book *O que é isso companheiro?* (Gabeira, 1996).
27. Oliveira (1991, p. 229).
28. According to the Curitiba-based journalist Luiz Geraldo Mazza, the original IPPUC team was heavily influenced by Lebret's ideas, which were for them (IPPUC), he says, "like a Bible." Mazza cites one particular Lebret statement that served as a motivation to the young urban planners in Curitiba: "Development is continuous and indivisible. It is necessary that all partial developments be integrated. If there is industrial and agricultural development, but without cultural development and sanitation services, then there is no development at all, but rather the possibility of setbacks" (Mazza, 1992, pp. 21–23).

29. The most cited example to illustrate the degree of popular suspicion that initially surrounded city hall proposals was the creation, in Curitiba, of Brazil's first pedestrian mall in the heart of downtown. As part of an ample urban renewal project, one that included public works and also the preservation of historic buildings, Mayor Lerner, in 1972, laid out plans to prevent car circulation on Curitiba's main street and Rua XV de Novembro. The reaction of shopkeepers was extremely negative, as they expressed concerns that customers would disappear with the traffic prohibition. Anticipating heavy business losses, merchants threatened to sue city hall and for sometime the whole city remained in suspense, observing the stalemate. Mayor Lerner decided to face the challenge and directed city workers to start the job on a Friday night. During the weekend, they removed the pavement, laid cobblestones, planted trees, created flowerbeds, installed benches, kiosks and ornamental streetlights, transforming the busy and disorderly street into a pleasant and colorful boulevard. Sometime later, the automobile club tried to retake the street for cars, but the attempt failed, as the residents were already getting used to the free walking on Rua XV. Today, more than 20 downtown blocks in Curitiba are closed to car circulation; the pedestrian corridors, contrary to the expectations of some, have re-energized the commerce and saved the city center from urban decay.

30. In *Memória da Curitiba Urbana* (1992, p. 7).

31. In *Memória da Curitiba Urbana* (1992, p. 3).

32. Peterson (1981, pp. 132–134).

33. Brasileiro Anisio (1999, pp. 461–462).

34. The local business class gave unconditional support to the creation of the industrial city officially inaugurated in March 1975. Conceived as a new community, with specific areas for housing, shopping, schools and factories, the industrial city through the years became a new locus for industrial projects, as multinational firms were attracted by the local infrastructure, in terms of roads and access to public transportation. Successive municipal governments in Curitiba have benefited from the industrial city's growth, as municipal revenue has increased, thus providing an essential backing to the city's urban development process. The evolution of the industrial city and its success is due to a well-articulated partnership between local

public officials and the local economic elite, an alliance to be seen, ultimately, under the logic of capitalism. The local entrepreneurs adhered to the urban planning process as it represented a conduit to foster business interests, including the benefits provided by the expected arrival of foreign investment. As a result of the 1964 military coup, the new authoritarian regime put in place an ambitious national development plan in which industrialization had a major role. The country's modernization plans contemplated massive investments in infrastructure, including new highways, power plants, steel production, and shipyard facilities which, to become a reality, would require the participation of the domestic industrial sector, in association with foreign investors. As the pace of urbanization was increasing, the metropolitan areas were the main focus of the new development strategies and the most logical choices for the creation and expansion of industrial projects were cities like São Paulo and Rio de Janeiro. In Curitiba, the local entrepreneurs soon realized that their moment to ascend to new heights had arrived, and that they could achieve the relevance and influence enjoyed by counterparts in the other two major state capitals. At the same time, Curitiba's entrepreneurs also reached the conclusion that to put the city on the map of central government policymakers, in terms of new investment—both domestic and foreign—a major local enterprise had to be undertaken: the chaotic state capital, living without a reliable public transportation service, with an inadequate road system and troubled by constant floods would have to be revamped to be competitive. Otherwise, Curitiba was destined to never leave its position of a large, yet provincial, city capital.

35. Material provided by Dennison de Oliveira, who was interviewed in his office at the Curitiba Federal University.
36. See Oliveira (1995, p. 209).
37. As published in a local newspaper.
38. During the administration of Mayor Fruet (1983–1985), Curitiba city council rejected an executive proposal dealing with the identification of idle urban areas, which would be subject to an extra tax. Alleging attempts to interfere with property rights, the Construction Industry Union (SINDUSCON) convinced the local legislature to repeal the mayor's project (Oliveira, 1995, p. 246).

39. See Souza (2001) for an account of urban reform in Brazil.
40. The Curitiba Industrial City (CIC) was given preference for new foreign investment that was vied by many other state capitals. The engineer Karlos Heinz Rischbieter, one of IPPUC's founding fathers and who later ascended to a high federal position, was behind the efforts to transform the CIC project into reality.
41. In *Memória da Curitiba Urbana* (1990, p. 18).
42. As a norm, housing programs in Brazil (even those managed by the municipal governments in large cities) have a federal component through the disbursement of funds. In the 1980s, with the dismantling of the Banco Nacional de Habitação (National Housing Bank), municipal housing programs, including those in Curitiba, suffered a major setback. Early in 2000, Curitiba city hall re-initiated the self-help construction projects.
43. CURA: *Comunidades Urbanas de Recuperação Acelerada* (Urban Communities of Accelerated Recuperation). The program was developed in the 1970s by the engineer Cássio Taniguchi, who years later, was elected mayor of Curitiba (2001–2005).
44. Excerpts of Lerner's political trajectory were provided by his advisor Jaime Lechinsky, who was interviewed by the author, in the Governor State House (Palácio Iguaçu), Curitiba, April 18, 2000. Mr. Brizola died in 2004.
45. In *Memória da Curitiba Urbana* (1991, p. 214).
46. Paranaguá Port Authority, on the outskirts of Curitiba, is operated by TCB, the leading container terminal operator in the Port of Barcelona.
47. Information provided by Dr. Rita Esmanhoto, former official at the Municipal Department of Health and currently faculty member in the department of Public Health at the Curitiba Federal University. She was interviewed in Curitiba on April 5, 2000.
48. In *Memória da Curitiba Urbana* (1991, p. 35).
49. See, for instance, Brasileiro Anisio (1999) and Hawken, Lovins, and Lovins (1999).
50. Oliveira (1995, p. 304).
51. See Hawken *et al.* (1999).

CHAPTER 4

WHAT HAS AILED
SÃO PAULO?

A great city is not to be confounded with a populous one.

—Aristotle

In January 2004, in the middle of a hot and rainy summer,
the city of São Paulo celebrated the 450th anniversary of
its founding—a landmark that city hall consciously used
to lift the self-esteem of *Paulistanos*. Concerts and other
cultural events, including multimedia displays, video docu-
mentaries and exhibitions of plastic arts, were organized
during that month—and some even stretched throughout
the year—to honor a metropolis that despite many ills can
be, at the same time, very welcoming. Similar to other large

urban centers around the world, São Paulo is a huge paradox with legions of admirers and critics. It has been variously called *capital da solidão* (the capital of solitude); *a cidade que não pode parar* (the city that can't stop); *São Paulo, meu amor; São Paulo quanta dor* (São Paulo, my love; São Paulo, so much pain); *locomotiva do Brasil* (Brazil's loco-motive); *cidade de muros* (city of walls); *a metrópole do medo* (city of fear); *coração do Brasil* (the heart of Brazil); *mãe, madrinha* (mother, godmother); *terra do dinheiro* (land of money); *São Paulo da garoa, São Paulo terra boa* (São Paulo of drizzles, São Paulo of good land). Two Jesuit adventurers who landed in Brazil in the 16th century founded the city. Manoel da Nóbrega and José de Anchieta[1] chose a plateau about 60 km from the Atlantic Ocean and established a mission to evangelize and educate the native population. On January 25, 1554, Nóbrega and Anchieta celebrated the first mass in the new but modest Jesuit College of São Paulo, in honor of Saint Paul's day of conversion to Christianity. That place became the ground zero of a city that almost five centuries later is one of the world's largest metropolises.

THE MAKING OF A METROPOLIS

The city remained a dusty and unimportant town until the late 19th century, when the abolition of slavery and the country's engagement with the international political and economic forces of the day changed the fate of São Paulo. In desperate need of new sources of labor, the newly instal-led republican government turned to immigration to replace the former slaves who had toiled in the coffee plantations or served as domestic servants in the São Paulo mansions owned by the *barões do café*, the coffee barons. Europeans came in droves, and São Paulo, a relatively small city at that time, opened its arms to them. The early waves of immigration were also the starting point of the Brazil's process of industrialization, which began in São Paulo. Industrialization triggered an unplanned and uncontrolled process of urbanization under the popular slogan that the city of São Paulo was like a mother's heart—it could always fit one more. Throughout the 20th century, the city grew in size, attracting intellectuals and investments from abroad, and by the late 1960s, it had been transformed into a metropolis with the arrival of the automobile industry in Brazil. Multinational companies built dynamic factories and created thousands of blue-collar jobs on the outskirts of São Paulo. However, at the same time, the seeds of malaise were being planted, and an uneasy feeling developed that the city was getting sick.

By 1965, such concerns led the architect Jorge Wilheim, an urban affairs specialist and former planning secretary for both the state of São Paulo and the capital city, to become deeply involved in the elaboration of São Paulo's master plan.[2] For Wilheim, the adoption of a rational urban planning strategy in São Paulo was a matter of life or death. The last meeting of the city hall planning commission had taken place in 1961, and the body laid dormant for several years thereafter due to a lack of interest on the part of the mayor. Wilheim and his colleagues from Brazil's Architects Institute (IAB—*Instituto de Arquitetos do Brasil*) were so concerned with the situation that they decided to invest in an advertising campaign under the slogan, "São Paulo needs a master plan." They pushed the idea that a planning instrument and new policies toward urban reform were an urgent necessity that required the collective action of professionals. Wilheim and several other urban planners, architects, and sociologists were witnesses to the city's chaotic urbanization process and were predicting more chaos to come.

At the same time, Wilheim was skeptical about the prospects of a new master plan for São Paulo, not because the city did not need it but mainly because of a general lack of an urbanistic vision among the country's ruling class. On many occasions he stressed how little understanding there was about urbanization processes in Brazil, observing in 1965, for instance, "we think that, within the limited scope of urban studies in Brazil, any work, even if a mere analysis of a urbanistic problem—if well framed—might contribute to reduce the alienation of our intellectual production and also to increase the knowledge of our reality... It is unbelievable that in a country with such intense spontaneous urbanization, we never have in our schools studies and examples drawn from this rich experience. On the contrary, we are immersed (and in a way quite static and formal) into the description of European medieval cities."[3]

Despite his skepticism, Wilheim felt that the mid-1960s provided a good opportunity to give São Paulo a new direction and to prepare it for the future. With the foundation of Brasília in 1960, Brazilians were getting their first sense of a comprehensive urban planning experience; according to

Wilheim, the new nation's capital provided some incentive for the development of new studies about the conditions of Brazilian cities in general. São Paulo was also just at the beginning of its metropolitanization process and had time and room to address imbalances. In view of his studies of the patterns of associational life in São Paulo, Wilheim had in mind a master plan that would respond to the residents' needs and activities. The plan included recreational clubs, country clubs, and open spaces for public meetings and for what he called "passive" arts and spectacles such as movie theaters and soccer games. São Paulo, Wilheim said at that time, "needs urban spaces for civic meetings." There were to be special spaces for street markets, the public sector would play a role in providing for urban recreation and, in response to a critical need, a new public transportation system would be implemented. São Paulo's mass transit at the time was not simply inadequate; it also failed to perform the crucial social function of integrating the urban space.

By 1964, when the IAB organized a seminar to discuss urban reform,[4] public transportation in São Paulo was teetering from one improvised solution to another as efforts to solve a given problem only created new ones because of a lack of overall planning. As a result of population growth, inadequate infrastructure and a real estate boom, the urban environment was deteriorating, green areas were disappearing, and the increasing use of cars was clogging the main streets. Wilheim[5] observed that "in lieu of a city planned for the full utilization of its environment and joy of its users, we find a metropolis without personality, ugly, denatured... In lieu of a place that symbolizes the cultural achievements of a society, we find 550 squared kilometers of real estate speculation, the paradise of urban lots that mutilated the natural landscape without adding any human value. How did we arrive at such degradation?" "Desamor," or lack of love, was the answer he gave. For Wilheim, the lack of love for São Paulo could be seen in the residents' careless attitudes regarding the "public good," in the contempt of popular opinion for the city council, in the *Paulistanos*' ignorance about their own city and in the local authorities' disregard for the urban space. Matters were made worse by the very important fact that the political and economic elites did not possess an urban vision for the country.

São Paulo's transit system was undermined by a chaotic road design that did not take into consideration the city's hills-valley-hills topography. Although the need to set aside more land for green areas had long been recognized, little was done to address the situation. A 1949 city government report had predicted that by 1970, large-scale land expropriations would be required to bring the green area per capita even to 2–6 square meters (the international standard recommends 16 square meters per inhabitant). However, by 1965, the only urban parks in São Paulo were those created before 1930 (the Ibirapuera Park, the city's most famous, remained unfinished until the 1960s). Wilheim noted that Vila Prudente, a São Paulo neighborhood with almost 200,000 residents, had no green areas at all. However, given the amount of empty land in the city, urban experts believed the issue of creating green areas could be resolved provided that an appropriate planning proposal was adopted.

Participants in the 1964 seminar hoped that their work would lead to the implementation of a new master plan that would transform São Paulo into a more humane and even pretty city. Transportation, land use, housing, and downtown renewal were critical priorities in this effort. The main objective of the mass transit proposal was to reverse municipal policies that made the city center the only hub for buses and streetcars. Passengers were forced to go downtown to transfer to another bus line going toward the neighborhoods. Urban experts had warned that a metropolitan mass transit system with a single center was unworkable, and their advice was proving to be correct. As part of the master plan, Wilheim and his colleagues proposed a polycentric transit and transportation system similar to those of London and Paris, where roads and avenues were designed to move traffic around the city and not just in and out of the center. São Paulo has a low degree of housing mobility as residents do not move very often, and a transportation system built around multiple metropolitan centers would connect residents to commercial sectors more efficiently.[6]

The proposed plan sought to improve transportation within the downtown area as well. Despite its concentration of historic buildings and financial institutions (including the country's major stock exchange and the headquarters of several commercial banks), the downtown area was dirty, congested, and dilapidated. Wilheim and his colleagues planned on prohibiting parking downtown and instead creating a ring around the city where individuals could park their cars and then use cabs or microbuses for travel within the city center. Reducing car circulation within downtown would eliminate the need for new parking garages and make it easier to enhance the area's financial activities and preserve its historical structures such as the gothic-style Cathedral, an 18th century monastery (*Mosteiro de São Bento*) and a handful of 19th century residential buildings that had been transformed into offices.

Another aspect of the 1965 plan dealt with the rivers that cross São Paulo. It is especially unfortunate that little was accomplished in this regard as flooding problems remain unabated; population growth has resulted in increased water pollution and land along the rivers that could have been transformed into recreational areas have experienced environmental degradation instead.[7] Wilheim has cited the Moldava River in Prague as an example of the extraordinary possibilities that an urban river could offer: several bridges allow for both commuting and leisure; the banks are now pleasant recreational sites; it is possible to go swimming and rowing in certain areas; and there are even ducks and swans around. Under these conditions, as he has stated, "Prague is one example of a complete and happy integration between a river and a city and with the life of its inhabitants."

In contrast, one of the rivers that cross São Paulo, the Tamanduateí, has been running for decades without treatment, and it receives the waste of at least 300,000 residents. Wilheim had already recorded the high levels of pollution in the river by 1965. Over the subsequent years, the situation deteriorated further for the Tamanduateí and two other rivers: the ample Tietê and its short tributary, the Pinheiros. Highly polluted rivers are nothing new in São Paulo, and the degradation is above all the result of government omission. A 1950 report noted, for instance, that already in 1890 a new government policy had been designed to clear the Tietê and Tamanduateí; a commission was created with the objective to go ahead with some work, but the public agency was dissolved in 1908 due to a lack of resources. The government did not resume attempts to rescue the city's rivers until 1923, and some sections were slowly recuperated by 1942. Nevertheless, the rivers have never received any comprehensive treatment, and no urban planning project was ever designed for the areas surrounding them.[8]

In the beginning of the 21st century, the Tietê, the Tamanduateí, and the Pinheiros remain highly polluted, and their recuperation seems decades away. The urban planners involved in the elaboration of the 1965 master plan presented several ideas to improve the rivers' conditions and to enhance the valleys where they are situated. Wilheim recalls that in the 1960s, a considerable part of the valleys was empty land, and he suggested that the city executive propose legislation for land use in those areas. With the support of federal resources, local authorities could have developed housing projects and recreational centers (parkways) along the rivers' banks.

A more ambitious idea was to make the Tietê navigable again, as it was in the 19th century. Over the years, pollution levels have prevented any kind of navigation, recreational or commercial, although the latter could generate important benefits as a considerable amount of nonmetallic minerals are produced in localities along the river. Furthermore, due to the high costs of dredging, very little has been done to alleviate the flooding problem. A lack of urban planning in the surrounding areas has transformed the banks into garbage deposits and a site for filthy and unhealthy human settlements. Moreover, local authorities have succumbed to financial pressures, and public land located near the rivers has been left to real estate speculation, especially for the construction of office buildings. This has eliminated any possibility of generating new green areas for the city, intensified traffic problems, and aggravated the housing shortage.

Almost four decades after the presentation of that comprehensive proposal for urban reform, the economically and politically mighty São Paulo is still suffering the consequences of misguided urban policies. The lack of governmental action at the local level can be explained in part by the country's tumultuous years after the 1964 military coup. A few months before the military took power, the federal government had time to create the Urban Policy Council, following suggestions coming from a seminar on urban reform that took place in July 1963.[9] The new federal agency, linked directly to the presidency, focused on implementing national urban policies to deal with the country's economic and social expansion. However, the coup d'etat effectively ended this effort and brought the nation to near paralysis as governors, mayors, and the society in general were left to wait for new directives coming from the group in power.

Despite being under authoritarian rule, governors and mayors were still elected by popular vote during the first years of the military regime, although only two parties were allowed to compete: the pro-military ARENA and the so-called "reliable opposition," the MDB.[10] In 1967, São Paulo's residents elected a new mayor, Brigadeiro José V. Faria Lima, who ran on a platform stressing "São Paulo Must Stop," in opposition to the grandiose slogan of the 1950s, "São Paulo Cannot Stop." Mayor Faria Lima did not embrace the proposed 1965 master plan in its entirety, but he recognized the need to control city growth. His freedom of action, however, was quickly limited when the military government adopted a much more hard-line stance in 1968 to suppress opposition. The national congress remained closed for a time and elections for state governor and state capitals mayors were suspended by decree.

With this "coup within the coup" (as the 1968 government crackdown was called), the military put the country on hold again. The darkest period of the dictatorship had begun, and it would slowly recede only in the early 1980s with the gradual process toward a democratic transition. Mayor Faria Lima left city hall in 1969 and was succeeded by the appointment of Paulo Salim Maluf. The new mayor was a successful businessman from a traditional Lebanese family that many years earlier had immigrated to Brazil. Maluf had no experience in politics or city administration. His family had built an industrial complex in São Paulo, and at the time he became mayor, Maluf was head of Eucatex, a family-owned, export-oriented wood paneling manufacturer. Although his tenure at São Paulo City Hall launched a political career that included a stint as state governor and a failed candidacy for presidency, Maluf's leadership was disastrous for São Paulo.

Other factors in addition to the authoritarian takeover contributed to Brazil's chaotic urban development process as well. Cândido Malta Campos Filho, an urban planner, architect and a faculty member at the University of São Paulo, emphasizes the absolute incoherence between the country's economic and urban policies and suggests that industrialization in Brazil, as it was conceived and as it is still taking place, has been incompatible with city planning.[11] He maintains that national policymakers undermined the prospects for city planning by making the automobile industry the pillar of the country's industrialization. São Paulo stands as an exemplary case of this contradiction. To sustain automobile production, urban policies have promoted cars as the mode of locomotion instead of focusing on developing the kind of reliable mass transportation system a city like São Paulo requires.

As a result, strategies to change the urban space are hindered by the increasing use of cars. Streets are becoming more congested; the city is becoming more polluted; and major public works to improve the flow of traffic are implemented without consideration for recreational and green areas, affordable housing projects or the need to control—or at least to reduce—the flooding problem. Buses often travel at less than 10 mph, and to save money, an increasing number of working people are commuting on foot. In São Paulo walking, driving and mass transit account for nearly equal thirds of the total commuting. In comparison, more than half of city trips in Paris and London are by public transport—either buses or subway.[12] Although São Paulo's subway has 4 relatively small lines, the number of metro lines in Mexico City and New York City are 8 and 25, respectively.[13] There is a consensus among urban experts that the cooperation of the upper classes will be essential to solve the problem of traffic jams, as their use of automobiles is intense and has been aggravated in part by the existence of a "car cult" in Brazil. Yet as Malta Campos Filho has observed, to convince people to leave their cars at home, it is first necessary to present them with an alternative in the form of an efficient public transportation network. The latter will only become possible if a comprehensive city plan is designed and implemented.

GOVERNANCE STRATEGIES ADRIFT

From the late 1960s to the late 1980s, São Paulo's city government launched three separate city planning initiatives. This first was in 1968 during Mayor Faria Lima's term, the second followed in 1971 under Mayor Reynaldo de Barros, and finally, there was the 1988 master plan during the Jânio Quadros administration.[14] None of these plans, however, adequately addressed the city's woes—either because the policy proposals were misguided or vague or because divergences between the mayor and legislators prevented government action. Paulo Bastos, a São Paulo-based urban expert, has described the 1988 plan as being "nothing more than a piece of paper."[15] The document is seen as a mere collection of generalizations without any mechanisms for making it applicable or enforceable. One of its clauses asserts that improvements in environmental quality require more control over water, air, and visual pollution. Yet there are no recommendations as to how city officials should comply with these dispositions.

The São Paulo governments' unwillingness or inability to put in place a coherent set of urban development policies is not unique in Brazil. Although under the 1988 federal constitution, a master plan is mandatory for cities with more than 20,000 residents in reality city planning is not a priority for city halls. The architect Flavio Villaça argues that Brazilian politicians do not believe in master plans and have never wanted them. According to him, the majority of Brazilian cities remain without planning programs, and he observes that in São Paulo, "for more than twenty years, the Municipal Department of Planning elaborates and reelaborates, does and undoes, revises and updates city plans, but no mayor ever demanded a master plan. Following the general rule, the mayor completes his plan, sends it to City Council at the end of his term and the successor withdraws the project to make a revision… São Paulo, likely, will continue with the same routine of the elaboration of a master plan in each administration without approving any."[16]

In an interview with the *Los Angeles Times*, Wilheim explained that urban policies in Brazil fail to address the problems they are supposed to solve because "planning is not popular. It is seen as an imposition that hinders my freedom of growing and getting rich."[17] Bruno Barreto Padovano, professor of architecture at the University of São Paulo emphasizes that "no direct relationship between the activities of urban planning and population growth can be perceived in São Paulo's history."[18] Yet as observed by the magazine *Metropolis*, São Paulo, probably like no other city in the world, demonstrates the need for sound urban planning. If one lesson can be drawn from São Paulo's governments' practices, it is that "no city should grow so arbitrarily," according to the architect Oscar Niemeyer, the Brasília planner. The situation seems so hopeless that urban experts doubt whether an urban planning initiative would ever emerge as an important policy goal in Brazil's largest city. One failed candidacy for mayor illustrates the point.

Former faculty member at Harvard University and author of, among other books, *The Future of American Progressivism* with Cornel West, the Brazilian political scientist Roberto Mangabeira Unger decided to enter the 2000 mayoral race with bold proposals to address São Paulo's most pressing urban ills. Arguing at that time that "there is no solution without a radical circumvention of the automobile," Unger proposed a tax on car use within city limits, with the proceeds to be invested in public transportation. Free parking lots would be created on the city's outskirts where drivers would leave their cars and take the metro or bus. Unger also had in mind the regularization of shantytowns by granting property titles to residents and offering them training in popular methods of housing construction. He also contemplated the idea of multiple centers that Wilheim had proposed in the 1960s with the creation of parks and plazas in new city centers. Yet polls showed that only a few of São Paulo's residents would have supported Unger's candidacy. In the middle of the electoral campaign, his party cancelled the nomination convention, and Unger returned to Massachusetts.[19]

Smaller scale planning proposals have generally not fared any better than the three comprehensive planning initiatives of 1968, 1971, and 1988. From one administration to another, urban programs have started and died in a series of interruptions that has been highly damaging to the city. While Mayor Maluf, who took power in 1969, abhorred master plans, his focus on major road enhancement works was of debatable efficacy. Attempts during Mayor Luíza Erundina de Sousa's administration to implement sound urban planning proposals were derailed by internal government strife.[20] Moreover, there have been instances when the city legislature has blocked reform efforts by rejecting proposed planning projects. The result has been a series of isolated, sectoral, and ill-conceived policies that were implemented with a high degree of improvisation and which produced poor results in the end. According to an analysis from the São Paulo-based Pólis, one of Brazil's most authoritative research centers on urban policies, "the lack of continuity has appeared as a result of the politicization of the administration, a condemnable practice that goes against the public interests. It is a common practice that mayors, instead of displaying a real concern with city problems, seek, in fact, to annul the public policies of previous governments and initiate new ones to imprint their signature on the city. According to the groups we interviewed, this phenomenon is becoming rather common, causing a lot of damage to the city residents. In addition to the financial costs related to unfinished public works, the actions do not progress as they are disrupted in the next administration."[21]

Mayor Maluf entered into politics knowing that São Paulo was in the middle of a chaotic urbanization process and on an intense march towards metropolitanization. In the 1970s, the largest chunk of population growth took place in the city's peripheral areas. The lack of infrastructure and reduced land prices in these distant districts resulted in uncontrolled housing construction, both legal and illegal, on tracts of land that lacked proper documentation. (Conditions have remained essentially the same in these huge urban settlements where the poorest of society live with almost no infrastructure in terms of drainage and sanitation and highly inadequate provision of public services, especially regarding garbage collection and mass transportation.) Neglecting the urban development plan that had been considered by his predecessor, Mayor Faria Lima, Mayor Maluf decided to direct municipal investments to individual transportation projects, thereby leaving the mass transit system as a whole without a clear direction.

Some administrations have tried to introduce improvements to the city public transportation system. Both Mayors Mario Covas (1983–1985) and Luíza Erundina (1989–1992) initiated reforms aiming to alleviate public transportation bottlenecks. Yet the projects basically failed in large part because they were designed in isolation from other urban problems, such as the constant floods, which have never been completely addressed. Mayor Olavo Setúbal (1975–1979) tried to launch a program to canalize minor watercourses and transform them into large avenues. However, as Karla Cardoso de Mello has stressed, this kind of public work proved to be inefficient for São Paulo.[22] In fact, floods and the costs they inflict in terms of material and human losses, diseases, property devaluation, increased traffic congestion, and stalling of commercial activity are becoming more frequent. In 1979, São Paulo authorities registered 125 areas that were subject to flooding; this number increased to 300 in 1984 and 403 in 1990.

Press reports indicate that the canalization of watercourses and the construction of roads over them have been a trademark of practically all São Paulo governments in the last three decades. These programs have been presented as the solution to the flooding problem, as a way to improve traffic conditions and as a means to increase property and land prices. However, the results in most cases have been in flagrant opposition to the goals stressed in the official discourses. As Karla Cardoso de Mello[23] has observed, "the multiple municipal interventions over the years and by several administrations were far removed from the city needs. In fact the road system is more than often saturated and when a 'solution' comes to speed traffic, the car owners are satisfied. Yet solutions like these did not improve the public transportation system, there is more road congestion and the flooding headache remains."

The high degree of disorganization that characterizes the policy process in the city of São Paulo is in large part the result of the government's lack of direction. It is important to note that public policies are also influenced by other factors—for instance the intricate relationships between local governments in metropolitan areas such as São Paulo and Curitiba. Yet, metropolitan contagion, in which problems in one town, such as flashfloods, affect other neighboring localities, only confirms the need for some planning tool.[24] This is not to say that an urban development plan has some special power to address all urban woes overnight. In fact, plans should not be seen as solutions in and of themselves, so much as tools that are used to try to manage what will happen next. Planning can help businessmen, governments, managers, and others to deal with uncertainties; it can be useful for taking advantage of opportunities, avoiding errors, and coping with changes.

The lack of a coherent guideline to deal with challenges posed by a metropolis that generates about 10% of the country's GDP has produced confusing government responses to São Paulo's most pressing problems. According to a survey conducted by the think tank Pólis, São Paulo residents define as "alarming" the city's social deficit, represented by an inefficient public transportation system, housing shortages, and the sad spectacle of thousands living under bridges. In an analysis of the results, the think tank observes that one of the most striking aspects of the survey refers to the residents' perplexity in face of the city degradation.

The path dependence theoretical framework, claiming that the self-reinforcing nature of the policy process can make governments prisoners of unsatisfactory policies, can be useful in the analysis of São Paulo's erratic governance strategies. The city leadership's lack of a clear commitment to a program of urban reforms that is compatible to the scale and needs of the metropolis has been a notorious shortcoming of all São Paulo governments in the last four decades. Instead of a more public entrepreneurial approach in government matters, as displayed by several Curitiba administrations, São Paulo's municipal sector has demonstrated little ability to act coherently in the face of urban problems. Lacking a long-term, strategic vision to deal with the dynamics of a growing metropolis, those governments have failed to anticipate adequately a variety of distortions and shortages in public services. In many ways, São Paulo's governments have lost control of the urban space. The unreliable public transportation system, which has contributed to the atmosphere of violence in the city, illustrates city hall's impotence in dealing with a critical sector that should be a vital instrument of social policy.

The successive municipal administrations in São Paulo never exhibited the kind of dedication that is needed to change the urban space for the better. In some cases, government action has been taken according to the whims of highly personalistic mayors, such as Maluf and Quadros. In other instances, well-intentioned mayors, such as Mario Covas and Luíza Erundina, were unable to deal with ideological and personal disagreements among city public officials. Irrespective of the specific reasons for their failures, collectively they have governed in a manner that is practically the antithesis of a public entrepreneurial approach. They have exhibited an inability to seek a broad consensus to support urban reform and instead have taken a neglectful attitude toward the importance of public debates and educational campaigns to discuss what afflicts the city and how to plan for the future. They have negotiated poorly with private actors who influence the policy process, and they have tolerated the low performance of city agencies, despite the presence of knowledgeable professionals inside them.[25] As a result, very few city programs have produced the results one would expect; on the contrary, some programs have been abandoned by the same administration that initiated them, while others have been interrupted when a new mayor took over.

From Maluf's first term in 1969 to his second term in 1994, and later with his by-now infamous crony, Mayor Celso Pitta, no São Paulo administration was successful in changing the course of events in the city, and there is no evidence to support the notion that one or few of them ever tried. Through this period the city grew in size (though not in the explosive or catastrophic numbers as some had predicted) and sophistication with regard to everything that is privately provided: financial services with a proliferation of ATM machines, fancy shopping malls, fine restaurants, an explosion of cellular phones, internet cafes, and even private security guards in response to increasing urban violence.[26] Needless to say, these are services that only few can afford. Regarding public services, which are, according to the constitution, a municipal responsibility, the picture is much more dismal, both in the sectors explored by this book as well as in areas such as health care, municipal libraries, and road repair. In the year 2000, Mayor Pitta was replaced by Mayor Marta Suplicy, who was elected amid positive expectations after the fiasco of her predecessor. Suplicy brought Wilheim into the heart of her administration as the new secretary of urban planning. Moreover, his experience produced some fruits when in 2002 the city council approved a new strategic master plan for São

Paulo. Unsurprisingly, the blueprint has striking similarities with Curitba's master plan. Wilheim envisioned a recycling system for São Paulo that would create work opportunities for street collectors, thus helping to mitigate the huge disparities in income distribution; environmentalism emerged as a goal in the form of new spaces for green areas; and the plan contemplated creation of a municipal housing fund based on contributions from builders.

However, the Suplicy administration was partially undermined by the mayor herself. A member of one of the most prominent families in the country, she was often seen as either aloof or arrogant. Halfway through her term she was engulfed in a domestic battle with her husband, a high-profile senator, and after the ensuing divorce she married one of her advisors. In the end the public exposure of her marital troubles, according to some analysts, played a role in her defeat for re-election in 2004.[27] Although in power, Ms. Suplicy tried to implement a governance strategy based on popular participation with the goal of improving public policy formation. Yet in the end, participatory mechanisms, in the form of participatory budgeting where city residents cast a vote to determine city budget priorities, were replaced by consultation, and the mayor was accused of governing in a top-down fashion. Mayor Suplicy tried to reorganize the city mass transit system in 2003 with a plan to regularize the use of vans as a mode of transportation, but a great deal of conflict within the sector pitting van drivers against bus companies has not mitigated the hardships of the city's millions of commuters.[28]

Suplicy left city hall to her successor, Mayor José Serra, who then chose to run for governor of São Paulo state instead of completing his term. It was a successful bid for him, yet another setback for the city, as the policy environment continues to exhibit a familiar pattern of failure in which urban programs are either ill-conceived at the outset or not allowed to mature. There is still a lack of a fundamental comprehension regarding what the city is now, where it is going or should go, and how to govern it. The Brazilian environmentalist, Aziz Ab'Saber,[29] noted this lack of direction when he suggested that the city residents should look for another kind of public official to manage the affairs of the metropolis:

> Any mayor or candidate for the municipal executive post should have a good and permanent notion of the impact of on-going projects on the city. And they should be able to sort out priorities and anticipate the chain of events of those projects. A viable candidate for São Paulo city hall should have a previous understanding of some basic questions affecting this big city. I am talking about the urban structure, the social composition of the urban fabric and its environs. Also, and most of all, it is about the functionality of the city and its formidable imperfections. Lastly, his knowledge should also incorporate an understanding of the metabolism of the urban organism and its customary and periodical spasms that afflict the urban ecosystem.

IS IT ALL ABOUT PLANNING?

In the last four decades, different São Paulo governments had the opportunity to work with four urban development proposals, in addition to a number of sectoral plans in the areas of public transportation and housing. None has ever been fully implemented, either because the mayors showed no interest in the measures that were proposed or because disagreements inside the municipal government impeded their implementation. According to urban specialist Regina Monteiro, a member of the nongovernmental organization *Defenda São Paulo*, urban development plans have failed in São Paulo because of the lack of a pact or broad agreement among the society and the private and public sectors. She identifies the absence of public debates about the role of planning as one of the major reasons why Brazil's largest city lacks clear and well-defined urban policies.[30] The city has grown arbitrarily in part due to the prevalent culture in which politicians do not believe in master plans because they see planning as an imposition. In addition to the politicians, there are plenty of political commentators who tend to condemn urban planning as a "tool of the elites."[31]

However, in addition to this antipathy toward planning, São Paulo also lacks any tradition of a politics of consensus that would make governance more effective. The city's public transportation struggles illustrate this point. As in the rest of Brazil, private bus companies in São Paulo represent a powerful business class that can be difficult to deal with. Conflicts between São Paulo City Hall and the company owners regarding services and fares are frequent, and disagreements over these issues have never been satisfactorily settled. Instead of negotiating with the private sector to reach agreement on implementing transportation reforms, São Paulo city governments have acted in ways that increased the bus company owners' animosity. Furthermore, sometimes promising government reforms are eliminated by a new administration such as that occurred to the public-private partnership established by Mayor Luíza Erundina to improve mass transit. This arrangement was killed a few years later by her successor, Mayor Paulo Maluf.

The government decision to allow unregulated vans to flourish in the city is an example of the contentious relations between the public and private sectors in the area of public transportation. These vans are now carrying millions of passengers in São Paulo each year. Although some mass transit experts assert that incorporating smaller vehicles into the public transportation system in large cities might enhance overall service, in São Paulo, the use of unregulated vans has transformed a potentially attractive transportation alternative into a source of conflict. Fearing the competition, the powerful city bus lobby for years blocked government attempts to legalize the new mode of transportation. This opposition resulted in an unregulated system of private van transportation that operated without guidelines in terms of routes and fares. The fact that city hall was reluctant to approach the private sector to discuss the introduction of vans into the public transportation system increased the atmosphere of mistrust and reduced the possibility that a productive public-private sector partnership could be created to help provide an essential service that affects the lives of millions. Whereas the van system has finally been legalized and is now regulated by city hall, it still remains a source of tension within the city. Van drivers, known as *perueiros*, operate the service in a mafia style that precludes proper oversight from the municipal authorities. Press reports suggest that some van companies may be involved with organized crime. Other companies have tried to create a parallel administration inside the municipal transportation system with the power to determine who can and who cannot request a license to operate a van. Violent and sometimes fatal disputes have broken out between *perueiros* as well.[32]

Although not without their own shortcomings, local governments in New York and Mexico City, North America's two other major metropolises, have been able to develop and implement successful transportation programs that incorporate several means of locomotion. Despite severe economic hardships, including a financial meltdown, currency devaluation, a recession and the devastating effects the 1994–1995 "tequila crisis," the subway remains a top priority in Mexico City. The underground network is in constant expansion and is among the world's largest systems.[33] (The São Paulo subway system, in comparison, is still one of the smallest among major metropolises.)[34] In Mexico City, privately owned minibuses, regulated by the local government, were for a long time the main providers of public transportation. However, since 2005, a modern publicly owned bus system, known as Metrobus and which was based on the model pioneered in Curitiba, has been in operation. By now at least 80 double-length articulated buses circulate on dedicated lanes along the city's most congested streets. Through several rounds of negotiations with the private minibus companies, Mexico City authorities secured their assent to the new mode of transport by offering the minibus owners either a partnership or a job with Metrobus.[35] Urban politics in Mexico City in terms of struggles within the city administration, disputes among political parties, influence peddling, clientelism, and mafia-style pressures are similar to those in São Paulo, if not more intense. Yet, politics itself is behind the determination to improve public transportation: realizing that the lack of adequate means of locomotion can create a social explosion and become a political liability, Mexico City governments have gone to great lengths to deal with the challenge posed by the daily mobility needs of millions of residents.[36]

Another essential public service, garbage collection, is a further example of how little São Paulo governments have done in terms of generating public support for municipal programs. In some measure, it is also the flip side of the contentious relations between the public sector and private interests described above concerning public transportation. In the case of garbage collection, collusion between government officials and private firms has resulted in corruption and bribery. There is a widespread perception among São Paulo residents that they do not have a voice in city hall's deals and decisions related to public services in general. Numerous press reports have documented several instances of governmental neglect in face of the population's complaints about mountains of trash proliferating on the streets. The garbage clogs public water drains and aggravates the flooding problem. Ignored by city authorities, residents have less incentive to do their part as far as the cleanliness of the city is concerned. Furthermore, city administrations have not made a comprehensive effort to educate the population regarding the public health consequences of garbage buildup. Solid waste separation and recycling are still in a very incipient stage.

To make the situation worse, the public-private partnership in São Paulo's garbage collection sector has been something of an urban nightmare. A major scheme of corruption and bribery was exposed involving government authorities, city council members, and the firms hired by city hall to collect garbage and mechanically sweep and wash the city streets. Whereas this collusion created a lucrative business for certain government and nongovernmental actors, the population did not reap any of the benefits that the arrangement was supposed to deliver. A two-year long investigation disclosed several irregularities in the services provided by the private companies, which systematically violated the terms of 14 contracts signed in the mid-1990s during Mayor Maluf's administration. It was revealed that the firms were paid for services they never performed. To avoid penalties, the companies gave thousands of dollars to city council members who had access to city hall accounting documents. The bribed legislators impeded the efforts of city employees to inspect and audit the work of the garbage collection companies. Instead of exercising their accountability duties and overseeing the performance of the municipal executive agency, the local assembly spent years involved in racketeering, apparently with the knowledge of the mayor. There were also fraudulent contract alterations, which increased the original payment of US$200 million to more than US$500 million to the private corporations in charge of the city janitorial services.

The shortsighted assessments in the case of public transportation and the bribery and rigged contracts in the garbage collection programs are just two examples of public-private relationships fraught with influence-peddling schemes. Several other irregularities have proliferated in São Paulo, particularly during the administrations of Mayors Maluf and Pitta. In general, São Paulo governments have never been willing or able to tap the impressive amount of resources in the hands of the city's private sector to improve the quality of services provided to the population. Summarizing what has been labeled the "municipal dirt," a 1999 editorial in *O Estado de São Paulo*, Brazil's most influential newspaper, asserted that, "a mafia controls the public services in the capital."

Is there a possibility of change? For the São Paulo-based economist Marcos Mendes, improvement in the city's governance strategies would require a new group coming to power that was committed to the city's well-being and that could pursue innovations in the delivery of public services. More attention must be paid to the distribution of public resources in a city with a large population and remarkable socioeconomic contrasts. (São Paulo has been described as "Belindia," a mix of Belgium and India.) Likewise, governance would be enhanced and governmental action made easier with the creation of organizations that specialized in urban functions and sectors. Additionally, according to Mendes, the success of governance practices is dependent on the ability of city hall to engage in productive negotiations with both political and nongovernmental actors—the city council, the professional associations, and the business class—aimed at the development of social projects and urban regeneration.[37] However, the pressing question is how?

Much has been said, although not in particular cogent ways, about the possibility that a city of 10 million inhabitants is simply ungovernable. Although it is not a trivial task to manage a metropolis of that size, it seems that the scale only becomes a problem when nobody takes care of it. São Paulo, in fact, appears to be much more of a case of an ungoverned than an ungovernable city. By dismissing several urban development proposals and only partially implementing various sectoral projects, its governments have demonstrated a basic lack of understanding of the city's dynamics, its growth process, and the need for well-crafted public policies to deal with its most pressing problems.

Several scholars affiliated with the São Paulo-based Fernand Braudel Institute have dedicated countless hours of study to discern how São Paulo governments could develop better governance practices. They have suggested, for instance, the creation of accountability mechanisms to deal with government corruption, something that is endemic in São Paulo and includes not only certain city councilors and city agency officials but also even a few employees of the *Tribunal de Contas do Município* (the municipal audit office). Ironically, this organization was created with the sole objective of auditing city government accounts. Other ideas include a revision of Brazil's system of federalism to promote more intergovernmental cooperation in the metropolitan area and even giving São Paulo city the status of a state.[38]

Regardless of the practical and political viability of these proposals, there is, however, a clear understanding among, or a common ground uniting, those concerned with São Paulo's direction in the 21st century: urban reform requires an institutional framework to support the changes. Norman Gall, from the Fernand Braudel Institute, is among those who see the urgent need for a major overhaul in São Paulo city government. If inaction persists, he predicts "São Paulo could stagnate and resign itself to poverty and disorder, abandoning its role as one of the world's great cities. We know by now that there is no perfect and final formula for administrative reform in big cities. We must follow a pattern of continuous evolution and adaptation to manage problems of scale and strengthen local responsibilities."

ENDNOTES

1. Nóbrega was a Portuguese Jesuit priest and first Provincial of the Society of Jesus in colonial Brazil. José de Anchieta was a Canarian Jesuit missionary. In addition to the foundation of São Paulo in 1554, both were also involved in the catechesis and conversion to the Catholic faith of the Indian population; their efforts at their pacification were crucial to the establishment of stable colonial settlements in the new country.

2. Personal meeting with Jorge Wilheim, who was interviewed in his São Paulo office in May 2000.

3. See Wilheim (1965, pp. 25–26).

4. The seminar took place in November 1964 with the participation of 120 urban planners, geographers, and architects. The topic was "The Man and the São Paulo Landscape." The conclusions served as basis for the master plan proposal.

5. Wilheim (1965, p. 62).

6. Several factors contribute to this lack of housing mobility. There are cultural aspects as families, especially those of Italian origin, prefer to live together or very close to relatives; in addition unemployment, other financial considerations and a chronic shortage of affordable housing also prevent that families move from one place to another with more frequency.

7 For the engineer Julio Cerqueira Cesar Neto, two factors explain why the flood problem remains unsolved: lack of planning and the careless government attitude regarding city cleaning and waste management. Constant flooding has afflicted São Paulo for more than a century. On January 8, 1879, *A Província de São Paulo* newspaper published that "as a result of torrential rain from 2 to 6 a.m., the rivers and creeks overflowed, transforming into superb lakes the areas surrounding the Tamanduateí and Tietê rivers, producing some damage." Many years later, after a quite number of municipal administrations, a 1997 survey detected 437 flooding areas in the city. Population growth and economic development triggered in São Paulo a chaotic process of land occupation, with people settling and erecting precarious houses

in areas where human settlements should never be allowed, such as on the banks of rivers and of important water reservoirs, as is the case with the Guarapiranga Lake in the city's south. Entire populations are at permanent risk as a result of floods. At the same time, human waste and garbage thrown directly into the watercourses are greatly undermining São Paulo's water supplies. The flooding problem is aggravated by the impermeability of São Paulo's terrain, preventing that the natural drainage of rainwater. Too little, too late, Mayor Celso Pitta developed a plan to build "swimming pools," which were, in fact, reservoirs to retain rain water. However, at the end of his administration, only two pools had been constructed, although the scale of the problem demanded many more. For Cerqueira Cesar Neto, incompetence is the root of problem. He says, for instance, that it is unthinkable that a downtown tunnel, *Túnel do Vale do Anhangabaú*, was built without a proper drainage system. As a result, when it rains, the tunnel becomes a dangerous river, trapping cars that within minutes are floating to the despair of drivers and passengers. "This is lack of institutional planning," the engineer says, adding that São Paulo government should also launch a public campaign raising awareness about the importance of keeping the city clean to allow for continuous water flow; garbage accumulated in city creeks also retains water that should go to the rivers. As a result, city streams overflow during the rain, causing floods in the surrounding areas.

8. Lysando Pereira da Silva, *Relatório da Comissão de Melhoramentos do Rio Tietê* (São Paulo, 1950).

9. The seminar was held in São Paulo and in Petropólis, near Rio de Janeiro, in the presence of 100 urban planners.

10. ARENA, Alliance for National Renewal, supported the military; MDB, Brazilian Democratic Movement was the opposition. With democratization, several others political parties are now competing in Brazilian politics. ARENA and MDB have changed their names.

11. During an interview in his São Paulo office, June 2000.

12. See Rotela (2001) for an interesting account of traffic problems in São Paulo. See also Mello (1998, p. 112) for a discussion on commuting on foot in São Paulo.

13. The subway in São Paulo is expanding thanks to investments made by the state government.

14. In 2000, Mayor Marta Suplicy and her secretary of urban planning, Jorge Wilheim, unveiled a strategic master plan that was approved by the city council in 2002. Suplicy's failure to win re-election in 2004 did not allow the plan to mature. Her successor, Mayor José Serra, left city hall much earlier than expected to run for state governor. He won, and became the governor of the State of São Paulo on January 1, 2007.
15. Interview for *O Estado de S.Paulo* newspaper, September 3, 2000.
16. Villaça (1995, p. 49).
17. See Rotela (2001).
18. As cited in Romero (2000).
19. In June 2007, Unger returned to Brazil to take a federal cabinet position as Minister of Planning.
20. Her administration was in part affected by a protracted conflict inside her political party, the Workers' Party (PT). Her election in 1988 was a significant achievement for the leftist PT, which was taking the command of the country's largest city. Luíza Erundina's victory represented a major challenge for the party, pitting militant PT members against PT government officials, both disputing what direction city hall should take. Her government was also marked by a great deal of governmental internal strife and lack of coordination among city agencies. Moreover, Mayor Luíza Erundina never was able to implement her project to decentralize the city administrative structure with the creation of subprefectures. According to Villas-Bôas (1996, p. 70), "the studies regarding the project of decentralization generated expectation and resistance inside the administrative machine, even before being discussed by the city council. The attempts to articulate the different groups inside city hall not always produced positive results, either because the bureaucracy remained tied to the centralized structure of the municipal sector, or because the political dispute that took place among those involved."
21. See Souto and Kayano (1996, p. 65).
22. Mello (1998).
23. Mello (1998, p. 85).
24. The metropolitan issue in Brazil is stimulating scholarly interest, due to its political, social, and policy implications. In the last few years, several studies have emerged pointing out the dilemma confronting

city governments in Brazil's metropolitan areas as a result of political and fiscal decentralization. At the same time that it is empowering local governments, decentralization is having a negative impact on public policy as governments in contiguous localities find it difficult to cooperate to solve common problems; for example, pollution control and mass transportation. Gall (2001) asserts that Brazil's new federalism has an "anti-metropolitan bias that neglects the big cities." His argument is that the country's 14 largest cities, which are state capitals in the center of growing metropolitan areas, have not benefited from an adequate level of federal transfers, whereas small towns in the Amazon region receive resources from the federal government corresponding to 10 times the local taxation. In this respect, it is important to note that following the 1965 master plan directives calling for a more harmonious development, governments of Curitiba, since the mid-1990s, have been seeking agreements with neighboring city halls to implement projects in public transportation and garbage collection.

25. The Pólis think tank, for instance, stresses in a study the "common-denominator" of São Paulo governments: the concentration of public investments in one segment of the city. The analysis compares Maluf and Erundina administrations: whereas the former made tunnels a priority, the latter paid attention only to peripheral areas. Therefore, the "sin" of both governments was "partiality," by focusing exclusively on one aspect of the urban space. Thus, according to Pólis, "both mayors Maluf and Erundina did not meet the expectations of a government focused on the city and citizens in its entirety" (1996, p. 65). São Paulo administrations have also showed little ability to seek some kind of consensus to facilitate government action. Villas-Bôas (1996), for instance, narrates serious divergences among public officials during Mayor Erundina's administration, and also constant fights between city hall and city council, leading to the derailment of environmental protection programs and of proposals to reorganize the city's administrative structures. As reported by Etienne and Zioni (1999), São Paulo governments never negotiated successfully with the bus company owners, a lack of articulation that explains the immobility of São Paulo mass transit. According to the authors, the public-private sector partnership "only brought disappointment"

(p. 182). There is no evidence that any city administration sought to instill in the society—as Curitiba governments did—the idea that the implementation of an urban development plan would be in the best interest of the city. Finally, despite its financial resources and fine urban planners, São Paulo governments have suffered from a damaging lack of organizational and coordination skills. Municipal departments and agencies have conflicting proposals to address the same problem, and it seems that city hall—administration after administration—cannot bring all them together or find a common ground. "Each agency has its own culture, nomenclature, and procedures and have nothing in common with other agencies," says Aldaíza Sposati, a former municipal secretary of regional administrations, cited in Gall (2001). In an example of how public agencies within the municipal government act as isolated entities that do not share information with each other, Gall observes that São Paulo Department of Finance simply cannot obtain information on property tax from the Department of Housing.

26. Public security, however, is not a municipal attribution in Brazil. The responsibility lies with states.

27. Stevens (2004).

28. Soares and Tavares (2007) expose some of the tactics of the van drivers, simply called *perueiros*, and their attempts to take control of São Paulo's public transportation system.

29. See Pólis (1996).

30. According to an interview in *O Estado de S.Paulo*, September 3, 2000.

31. São Paulo-based professor Ermínia Maricato views master plans as a policy tool in general designed for the official and not the real city. She condemns the so-called "Barcelona Model," by many accounts a sound urban development plan that some Latin American cities tried to emulate. Yet Professor Maricato rejects the Barcelona's option for its excessive focus on "the competitive city, the entrepreneurial city, the merchandise city, the city that many international consultants like the Catalans, use to present it with a left wing discourse, but sell it as a right wing project. A large part of the Latin American left, and even governments, ended up buying this rigmarole." However, Professor Maricato agrees that urban development plans

are necessary and important, provided that the program covers the entire city. (Fragments from Maricato's lecture, World Social Forum, Porto Alegre, Brazil, January 31-February 5, 2002).

32. Soares and Tavares (2006).

33. According to *Jane's Urban Transport Systems (2002–2003)*, the largest subway systems (by length) are: London, 415 km; New York City, 371 km; Moscow, 340 km; Tokyo, 281 km; Seoul, 278 km; Paris, 211 km; and Mexico City, 202 km. The Mexico City subway operates with funds provided by the federal government.

34. According to official information, the length of the São Paulo subway is 60.5 km and currently in expansion. The system is owned and operated by the government of the State of São Paulo.

35. A public opinion poll taken by *Reforma*, a Mexico City newspaper, revealed in July 2005 that 75% of Metrobus riders said they considered it better than the old minibuses. See Malkin (2005).

36. New York City has also tried the Curitiba model of public transportation in the 1990s (Gardy, 1998).

37. See Mendes (2001).

38. See Gall (2001).

CHAPTER 5

LESSONS FROM
THE URBAN LABORATORY

Being human is itself difficult, and therefore all kinds of
settlements (except the dream cities) have problems.

—Jane Jacobs[1]

In many instances, the assumptions in this book coincide
with the view expressed in the Jane Jacobs quote above in
the sense that there is not a perfect urban reform. Cities are
live organisms, and at the same time that some problems
are cured, others emerge as a result of urban dynamism.
City governments, despite their commitment to the public
good, will never be able to redress all the ills that afflict the
population, such as abject poverty or income distribution

disparities. The latter are major structural flaws rooted in the distortions of national political economies, which are in turn subject to the dynamics of global markets. Yet as Jaime Lerner—a renowned urban planner, former mayor and former governor—has stressed a long time ago, strictly within their sphere of action, municipal governments should be able to address the basic urban pathologies.

GOVERNMENT, POLITICS, AND URBAN VISIONS

By all indications, Curitiba's master plan has given its governments a sense of direction on how to conduct city affairs. Thanks to a sensible municipal strategy, urban programs have not been derailed as elsewhere in Brazil. This policy continuity has facilitated government action and produced more successful outcomes, and it is creating an urban development culture among the citizenry. By now, no aspirant to city hall can expect to be electorally competitive in Curitiba if his or her political platform does not include a clear commitment to the urban development process that has been in place for almost four decades. The satisfactory outcomes in public transportation and environmental management have not occurred by chance in Curitiba; on the contrary, they have to be understood in the context of an institutional framework conducive to better governance practices. In São Paulo, a chaotic policy regime has weakened government action and led to less successful outcomes. This has reinforced an almost sclerotic institutional framework that has made governments prisoners of damaging policies, and hence, of flawed governance strategies.

In Curitiba, institutional change toward a more harmonious policy environment that facilitates government action was achieved by the city governments' consistent commitment to the urban development process, by their ability to seek and obtain some degree of societal consensus through sustained negotiation processes, and by city hall's steady support for the IPPUC, a unique agency in Brazil for its centrality in urban policy. Deeply informed by the knowledge of seasoned professionals—town planners, engineers, architects, economists, and mass transit experts—the IPPUC has been, since its inception, instrumental for all Curitiba governments. Several decades of rigorous research (both in Brazil and abroad), the accumulation of experience, and the constant process of project testing have legitimated the agency as an authentic urban development authority that is the city hall's right hand.

Despite all its achievements, Curitiba's major lessons for the study of politics and government do not concern the successful urban program *per se*, although there is much to say about its positive impact on the public space. Rather, it seems to me that Curitiba's most important contributions derive from the ways in which its governments were able to attain those goals. It is by now recognized both in Brazil and abroad that the governance strategies in Curitiba have been quite successful in enabling its governments to deal with urban problems that seem to be almost intractable in many other cities. By refining continuously a broad planning instrument that goes beyond the technical characteristics of a conventional master plan to encompass a more inclusive urban strategy, successive Curitiba governments have developed and adhered to a strategy that guides a comprehensive urban development process, integrating public transportation, environmental management, and local economic development.

The implementation of this urban development plan, which evolved from a set of infrastructure projects to tackle, in the end, social concerns, did not take place by chance and nor was it the feat of a single government. The determination of a mayor who understood the need both for an urban development blueprint and a strategy to build support for its implementation was necessary at the very beginning. The mayor sought the support of—and in turn gave support to—a group of professionals who designed a plan that emerged as a policy instrument that included sensible guidelines to orient the city's growth. The entire team realized that the mere imposition of projects would likely result in failure, and they recognized that their proposals, which at the time were truly innovative, would need some degree of popular legitimacy if they were to be implemented. Thus, slowly, through negotiations with strategic private sector actors, particularly the bus companies' owners and the neighborhood associations, and with the help of media campaigns and public debates, the governing group was able to establish the pillars of a major urban reform.

Curitiba's urban development process is also an invitation to think in different ways about the nature of democratization processes. Despite the expectation of better governance practices, the democratic transition in Brazil has not produced, by and large, more responsive governments at the local level. This apparent contradiction does not seem to be exclusive to Brazil. The 2001 financial meltdown in Argentina was in part attributed to the fiscal irresponsibility of provincial governments that were empowered as a result of the country's democratization process that started in 1983. While democracy has to be defended by all means, one should not take it as the panacea for all national troubles. Rather, one should realize that regime change will not automatically increase a government's ability to govern better. Good governance strategies at the local level require political commitment, policy innovation, citywide negotiations, and organizational skills—all attributes displayed by successive governing groups in Curitiba. Their actions were guided by a planning instrument, which was neither static nor rigid, but was constantly revised by the IPPUC. The city's unique civic culture, shaped by the urban development vision that emerged in the 1960s, helped to glue all this together. By now Curitiba residents are well aware of how the urban planning process has improved service delivery and made municipal authorities more responsive to city needs. Curitiba is certainly not a dream city, as such a concept does not exist in reality. However, the urban development process in Curitiba illustrates the benefits of a well-articulated governance strategy and the positive outcomes of well-designed government interventions.

EPILOGUE

In summarizing the strategy that governments in Curitiba have followed to improve governance practices, Maria Rocio Morais do Rosário has said that "it is necessary to think in ideal terms and to perform in terms of what is viable," adding that what Curitiba's experience offers "is action today, yet with a long term vision."[2] This has been facilitated by an urban planning strategy without rigidities that consists of a set of feasible ideas for a more harmonious development, always taking into account the human and physical characteristics of the urban space. Moreover, Rosário emphasizes what has also been stressed throughout this study: to produce good results, urban policies have to be anchored in an institutional setting that favors them and that gives priority to innovative practices.

After almost four decades of a truly innovative urban experiment in the Brazilian context, the Curitiba case offers both reasons for concern and for optimism. On the one hand, the existence of urban programs with an actual positive impact on daily life has not, however, altered the reproduction of social inequalities, which are bitter realities for Brazilians in any part of the country. On the other, taking into account the contradictions that are inherent to any political process and considering the urban malaise that affects Brazil's large cities, Curitiba demonstrates that another course of action is possible. It has not been without imperfections, yet it has proved to be a sensible path to urban reform.

From a chaotic provincial city, deprived of infrastructure and plagued by unreliable public services, Paraná's capital has been transformed into a vibrant metropolis in possession of the best public transportation system in the country—and certainly among the best in the world. The municipal authorities have pioneered a recycling program for domestic garbage based on environmental protection, education and income generation, which has had far-reaching consequences. These programs are the highlights of a broad governance strategy that also includes the promotion of local economic activities—business incubators—which in turn spreads the benefits of urban development, such as services and infrastructure, to previously abandoned, neglected, and rundown areas of the city. In short, public policies in Curitiba are never taken in isolation, but rather they emerge in the context of a holistic urban planning process that deals with the city in its entirety.

Domestically and abroad, Curitiba's governance strategy has been recognized as quite successful, and as departing from the serious deficiencies that plague many other city administrations in Brazil. Over the years, public policies in Curitiba have produced favorable outcomes, which have facilitated official action, conferred legitimacy to governments and to some extent have made city politics more reliable. This self-reinforcing process has contributed to urban improvements, which the citizenry supports. This predictable policy environment is more likely to produce enhancements in the urban space than policy derailment—a common practice in Brazil. Thus, there is a degree of uniqueness in the urban development process in Curitiba; yet this does not mean that there are no generalizable lessons for those concerned with the quality of urban life and how to improve it. Cities are very peculiar organisms, with different sizes, shapes, economic profiles, politics, and above all, urban needs. However, there is one particular need that they all share: an urban vision.

ENDNOTES

1. Jane Jacobs (1916–2006) was an American-born Canadian urban planning expert, writer, and activist. She is best known for *The Death and Life of Great American Cities* (1961), a powerful critique of the urban renewal policies of the 1950s in the United States.
2. IPPUC official, as cited in *O Estado de S.Paulo* newspaper (2002).

ABRIDGED VERSION OF THE 1965 CURITIBA MASTER PLAN

The City Council of Curitiba, the capital of the Paraná State, has approved and I, the Mayor, sign the following Law:

CHAPTER I

PRELIMINARY CONSIDERATIONS

1. Hereby it is instituted the Curitiba Master Plan with all its Basic Guidelines, aiming to orient and control the integral development of the municipality.
2. The Plan aims to provide better conditions for a harmonious and comprehensive development and well being of the community and its metropolitan area.

3. To implement the Plan, the Mayor may sign agreements with any public authority at Federal, State and Municipal levels.

No changes, alterations in the Master Plan will be done without the legislature's authorization.

CHAPTER II

THE PLAN BASIC GUIDELINES

Section I

Road System

The Master Plan will determine the organization of the road system, which comprises:

> Federal and State Roads; Municipal Roads; Rural Ring; Structural Roads; Connecting Roads; Express Lanes; Central Ring; Connecting Roads between districts; streets, squares and boulevards preferably or exclusively for pedestrians.

Several following clauses describe new norms regarding the functions and dimensions of each type of road; the creation of special road crossings, the construction of new road accesses; outline how existing roads will be enhanced; and detail instructions regarding urban land expropriation to meet the plan's requirements.

Section II

Zoning

For the purposes of this Law, the municipality is divided in different zones, aiming at a harmonious development of the community and the well being of its inhabitants.

> For the purposes of this Law, the Municipality is divided in urban areas, areas of urban expansion and a rural area.
> The IPPUC will determine what will be the adequate urban solution for each zone.

Several following clauses describe new land use regulations regarding edifications; building licenses; areas that are off-limits for construction; specifics norms for construction in residential areas; guidelines for the installation of shops and factories and the prohibition of certain commercial activities that can put in danger the lives of residents; specific norms for industrial units; the powers of IPPUC to oversee the compliance of the law and other city ordinances.

Section III

Land Lots

> The opening of streets and other public places shall be done in accordance to this Master Plan and it always will be dependent on the municipal government's approval.

The following clauses stipulate the conditions under which public and private works will be conducted, taking into account first: that surface waters must flow freely; that construction is not permitted in green spaces; that construction is also forbidden in swamps and in areas subject to flooding, until adequate drainage works are completed.

Section IV

Urban Renewal

> Establishes an Urban Renewal Policy for the Municipality of Curitiba; the policy is defined as a system whose goal is to prevent urban decay; to recuperate precarious and declining areas; the policy is also an instrument to promote society well-being.

The following are the objectives of the Urban Renewal Policy:

1. To provide adequate destination to existing buildings, including the possibility that they recover their original use.
2. Reparation and recuperation of decadent buildings.
3. Reparation of buildings and other public spaces.
4. The utilization of urban land in accordance with the community's social needs.
5. Improvements and enhancements of existing buildings for public purposes.

Instruments for the implementation of the Urban Policy Renew:

a) The expropriation or acquisition of property, for public utilization or for social interest;
b) The construction and re-construction of roads, parks, public squares and other urban spaces;
c) Sale, concession or authorization to use property that has been acquired for social purposes;
d) Fiscal incentives as compensation to those who voluntarily repair and rehabilitate buildings;
e) Imposition of penalties in case of violations.

Several studies by the IPPUC will determine the areas subjected to Urban Renewal.

The costs of the public works will be defrayed with the creation of the Urban Renewal Tax.

Section V

Preservation of Traditional Historic Sites

> Establishes the Policy of Preservation of Traditional Historic Sites, in the Municipality of Curitiba, aiming to preserve the historical and urban values in certain areas

Objectives of Policy of Preservation of Traditional Historic Sites

1. The definition of urban phases.
2. If possible, to assure the immutability of buildings and other public facilities.
3. Recuperation of buildings, keeping the characteristics of a given historic period.

4. To promote in the historic sites, activities that are compatible with their characteristics.

5. Tourism promotion.

The IPPUC will define the Traditional-Historic Sites.

Section VI

Construction

> No building will be repaired or demolished without previous license granted by the respective municipal agency.
>
> All building projects shall be elaborated in accordance to this Master Plan.
>
> The constructions, repairs and demolitions or any other construction work made in disagreement with the basic norms of this Master Plan will be embargoed by the municipality.
>
> In accordance with the basic guidelines of this Master Plan, the construction regulations take into account conditions and technical norms that promote city development and the harmony of the urban environment.

Section VIII

Public Services And Community Facilities

All projects and implementation of public services shall be done in agreement with this Master Plan.

It is expressly forbidden, for either individuals or corporations, to deposit residues in waterways, lakes, and other water reservoirs in the Municipality.

The Municipality is being divided into Sanitary Sectors, whose jurisdictions will be defined by the IPPUC.

Each one of these Sanitary Sectors will have a Health Center.

The Sanitary Units will assist districts between 10 and 20,000 inhabitants; if possible, these units will be built close to public schools, aiming in the future the creation of community centers.

CHAPTER III

GENERAL DISPOSITIONS

Within 60 (sixty) days, the Mayor will send to the Local Legislature all regulations regarding Zoning and Urban Lots, in accordance to the basic guidelines of this Master Plan; within six months, the Mayor will send measures to amend the current Municipal Tax Legislation, in order to create incentives to implementation of this Master Plan, and the imposition of fines and penalties for the cases that violate these Basic Guidelines.

(Excerpts of Mayor's speech during the signature of the law, according to text included in the piece of legislation)

"...As a Mayor of Curitiba, I seek to address the most serious and pressing municipal problems, starting with Guidelines for General Action that later were transformed into a Governmental Planning Instrument..."

"Although I do not count with a political major-ity in the Municipal Legislature, but trusting in its members' civic spirit and sensibility regarding our collective problems, I submitted to the approval of City Council several bills aiming to equip City Hall with adequate tools allowing it to deal with municipal problems that pose a challenge to government action..."

"Hereby I stress the approval of several bills that created the Urbanization Authority (URBS); the Municipal Fund for Urbanization and Sanitation (FURBS); the Curitiba Popular Housing Company (COHAB-CT); and the Indigent Rehabilitation Foundation. And now, crowning an intensive legislative work, we have the Law 2828 that institutes the Curitiba Master Plan..."

10 of August 1966,
Liberdade Square, Curitiba
IVO ARZUA PEREIRA, MAYOR.
Source: Curitiba City Council, Law 2828, 10.Ago.1966
(Edited for the purposes of this book).

APPENDIX II

ILLUSTRATIONS

Illustration 1. Brazil map.

Source. Perry-Castañeda Map Collection, University of Texas Libraries.

Illustration 2. Tube station: A new concept of bus stop developed in Curitiba.

Illustration 3. Library: *Faról do Saber,* the "lighthouse of knowledge," which are small libraries that meet educational needs and also contribute to the revitalization of urban spaces. There are 54 such units in Curitiba.

Illustration 4. Master Plan in the news: In the 1960s, the innovative urban planning process in Curitiba was gaining attention nationally.

Illustration 5. Incubators: There are 12 entrepreneurial sheds in Curitiba; these incubators support the development of about 100 small businesses, contributing to local economic growth, job creation, income generation, and recuperation of rundown areas in the city.

Illustration 6. Environmental units in Curitiba: Each dot corresponds to a unit, formerly called PIA, to promote environmental education among the youth.

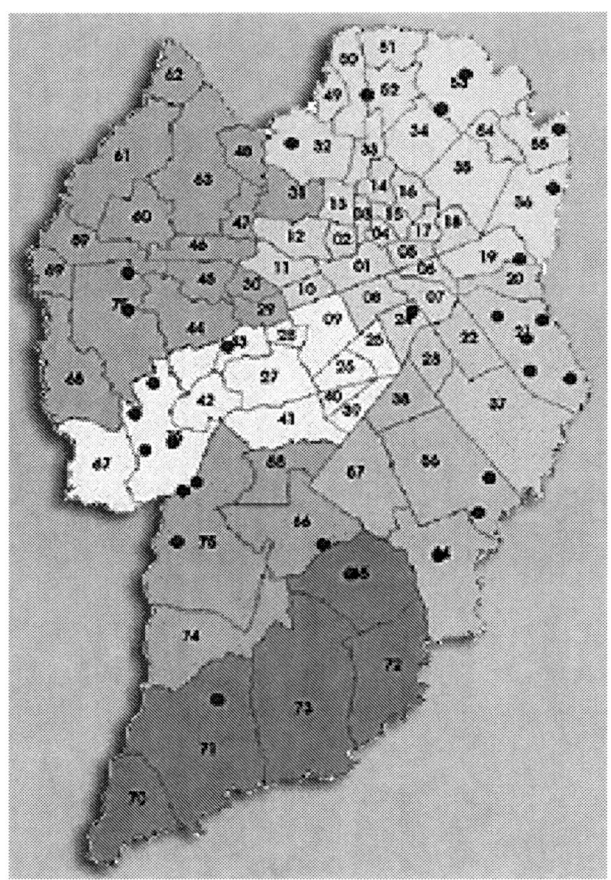

Illustration 7. Planning Commission: the origins in the 1960s of the commission that soon would become the IPPUC.

Illustration 8. Mass Transit Net: Curitiba's innovative and efficient bus system, now reaching the localities in the metropolitan area.

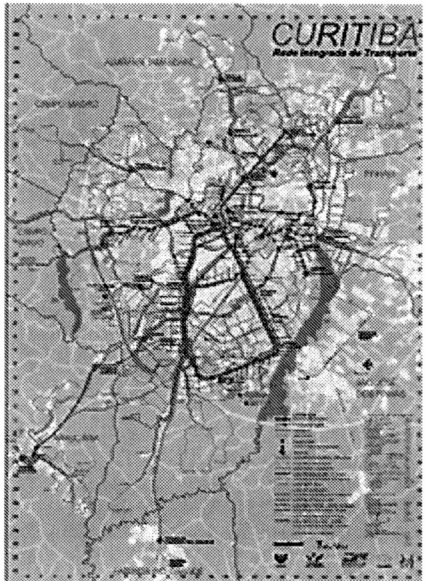

Illustration 9. Green Exchange: Each dot corresponds to a site where residents can exchange recyclable materials for bags of produce.

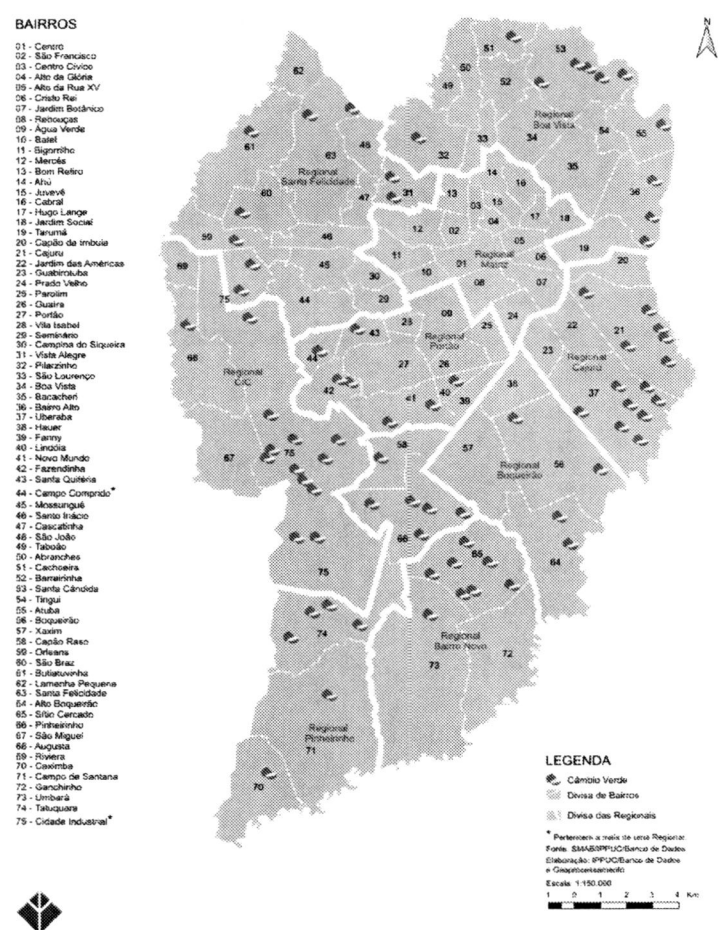

Programas Comunitários de Abastecimento em Curitiba
Câmbio Verde - 2006

Illustration 10. Environmental management: The Open Environmental University (top); trucks regularly collecting residential garbage for recycling (below).

Illustration 11. The Botanical Garden is one of Curitiba's most visited tourist attractions.

Illustration 12. Planning Curitiba.

Credits: Courtesy of the Institute of Research and Urban Planning of Curitiba (IPPUC) and Curitiba City Hall.

BIBLIOGRAPHY

Araújo, M. N. (1994). *Urban tree attitudes and comparison of tree survey methods in the city of Curitiba, Brazil.* Unpublished manuscript.

Assunção, L. F. (1999). Coleta Seletiva de Lixo Ainda é Sonho em SC. *A Noticia.*

Banfield Edward, J. W. (1996). *City politics.* New York: Vintage Books.

Bicalho, M. (1998). A Dívida Social no Transporte Coletivo. *Revista dos Transportes Públicos* (80), 33–41.

Bongestabs, D. H. (1983). *Curitiba: O Meio Ambiente.* Curitiba, Brazil.

Brasileiro Anisio, E. H. (Ed.). (1999). *Viação Ilimitada: Ônibus das Cidades Brasileiras.* São Paulo, Brazil: Cultural Ed.

Brugmann, J. (1996). Planning for sustainability at the local government level. *Environmental Impact Assess Review* (16), 363–379.

Brundtland Report. (1987). *Our common future.* Oxford, UK: Oxford University Press.

Building & Social Housing Foundation. (2000). *New Frontiers in Urban Governance.* Leicestershire: United Kingdom

Bushell, C. (1993). *Jane's urban transportation system.* Surrey, UK: Jane's Information Group.

Calderoni, S. (1997). *Os Milhões Perdidos no Lixo.* São Paulo, Brazil: Ed. Humanitas.

Cervero, R. (1995). *Creating a linear city with a surface metro.* Institute of Urban and Regional Development, Berkeley: University of California at Berkeley.

CNT. (2002a). *Importância do Transporte de Passageiros para a Eficiência Econômica e Mobilidade da População.* Brasília: Confederação Nacional do Transporte.

CNT. (2002b). *Transporte de Passageiros.* Brasília, Brasil: Confederação Nacional do Transporte.

Czarniawska, B. (2002). *A tale of three cities—or the glocalization of city management.* Oxford, UK: Oxford University Press.

Daily, G., & Ehrlich, P. (1992). Population, Sustainability, and Earth's Carrying Capacity: A framework for estimating population sizes and lifestyles that could be sustained without undermining future generations. *BioScience,* November, 1992.

Davidoff, P. (1996). Advocacy and pluralism in planning. In S. F. Campbell Scott (Ed.), *Readings in planning theory.* Oxford, UK: Blackwell.

DBJ (2000). Curitiba Ecocity: Personal Reflections on the Most Livable City in South America. [Electronic Version]. *Development Bank of Japan.* http://www.dbj.go.jp/english/IC/hot/curitiba/01.html#I

Dieguez, C. (2000). A Farra municipal. *VEJA,* July 26.

de Oliveira, D. (1991). O Campo do Planejamento Urbano em Curitiba. *História: Questões e Debates* (12), 220–238.

de Oliveira, D. (1995). *A Política do Planejamento Urbano: O Caso de Curitiba.* Unpublished

Dowbor, L. (1998). Decentralization and governance. *Latin American Perspectives, 25*(1), 28–44.

Eaton, K. (2006). Decentralization's nondemocratic roots: military reforms of subnational governments in Latin America. *Latin American Politics and Society, 48*(1).

Elkin, S., & Soltan, K. (1993). *A new constitutionalism* Chicago: University of Chicago Press.

Etienne, H., & Zioni, S. (1999). Ônibus na Metrópole: Articulações entre a Iniciativa Privada e Intervenção Pública em São Paulo. In H. Etienne, & E. H. Brasileiro Anisio (Eds.), *Viação Ilimitada: Ônibus das Cidades Brasileiras.* São Paulo, Brazil: Cultura Ed.

Fadel, E. (2001). Lixo de Curitiba Vira Acervo de Museu. *O Estado de S.Paulo,* August 14, 2001.

Farbman, D. (1960). *A description, analysis and critique of the master plan.* Philadelphia: University of Pennsylvania.

Fazio, J. (2002). Mayors support urban forestry. *Tree City USA Bulletin.*

Fernandes, A. (1990). Planejamento Urbano em Curitiba: A Institucionalização de um Processo. In *Memória da Curitiba Urbana* (vol. 4). Curitiba, Brazil: IPPUC.

Ferreira, M. C. (1999). Associativismo e Contato Político nas Regiões Metropolitanas do Brasil: Revisitando o Problema da Participação. *Revista Brasileira de Ciências Sociais, 14*(4), 90–101.

Fickett, A., Gellings, C., & Lovin, A. (1990). Efficient use of electricity. *Scientific American,* 28.

Figueroa, O. (1996). A hundred million journeys a day: The management of transport in Latin America's Mega Cities. In A. Gilbert (Ed.), *The mega city in Latin America.* Tokyo: United Nations Press.

Friberg, L. (2000). Innovative solutions for public transport: Curitiba, Brazil. *Sustainable Development International,* 153–156.

Fried, R., & Rabinovitz, F. (1980). *Comparative urban politics: A performance approach.* Englewood Cliffs, NY: Prentice-Hall.

Fruet, M. (1985). Curitiba Discute com a Comunidade. In *America Latina: Crises nas Metrópoles.* São Paulo, Brazil: SEMPLA.

Gabeira, F. (1996). *O que é isso companheiro?* São Paulo, Brazil: Cia. das Letras.

Galeano, E. (2001). *Upside down.* New York: Metropolis.

Gall, N. (2001). *Political disorganization and problems of scale: São Paulo Metropolis.* São Paulo, Brazil: Faculdade Armando Álvares Penteado (FAAP).

Garcia, F. S. (1997). *Cidade Espetáculo: Política, Planejamento e City Marketing.* Curitiba, Brazil: Palavra Ed.

Gardy, A. (1998). Hey New York: Listen up! 12 ideas from (gasp) out of town; looks like a bus, acts like a subway. *The New York Times,* September 6.

Habitat, I. (2005). History of the concept: Henri Lefebvre's "Right to the City" [Electronic version]. *Urban policies and the right to the city.* Retrieved March 18, 2005, from http://www.hic-net.org/articles.asp.

Hackenberg, D., & Andreiko, M. (2006). Faróis do Saber [Electronic Version]. *Patrimônio Paranaense*. Retrieved April 12, 2006, from http://www. abpr.org.br.

Hagopian, F. (1996). *Traditional politics and regime change in Brazil*. Cambridge, UK: Cambridge University Press.

Hall, P. (1982). *Great planning disasters*. Berkeley: University of California Press.

Harvey, D. (2003). The right to the city. *International Journal of Urban and Regional Research, 27*(4), 939–941.

Hawken, P., Lovins, A., & Lovins, H. (1999). *Natural capitalism: Creating the next industrial revolution*. Boston: Little, Brown.

Holli, M. G. (1999). *The American Mayor: The best and worst big city leaders*. University Park: Pennsylvania State University Press.

Holston, J. (1989). *The modernist city*. Chicago: University of Chicago Press.

IBGE. (1996). *Contagem Populational*. Retrieved from www.ibge.gov.br.

IBGE. (2000). Censos Demográficos—Características de População e Domicílios. Retrieved from www.ibge.gov.br.

Jacobi, P. (1997). Meio Ambiente Urbano e Sustentabilidade: Alguns Elementos para a Reflexão. In C. Cavalcanti (Ed.), *Meio Ambiente, Desenvolvimento Sustentável e Políticas Públicas*. São Paulo and Recife, Brazil.

Kirdar, U. (Ed.). (1997). *Cities fit for people*. New York: United Nations Publications.

Kreimer Alcira, T. L., Menezes, B., Munashinghe, M., Parker, R., & Preece, M. (1993). *Rio de Janeiro: In search of sustainability*. Washington, DC: World Bank.

Lapper, R. (2006). S. Paulo shows the way to civilise a mega city. *Financial Times*, August 24.

Lavoie, D. (1991). *Economics and hermeneutics*. London: Routledge.

Lebret, L. (1962). *Manifesto por uma Civilização Solidária*. São Paulo, Brazil: Duas Cidades.

Lefebvre, H. (1969). *El Derecho a la Ciudad* (J. Gonzalez-Pueyo, Trans., 1st ed.). Barcelona, Argentina: Ediciones Península.

Lefebvre, H. (1996). *Writings on cities* (K. Lebas, Trans.). Oxford, UK: Blackwell.

Levi-Strauus, C. (1999). *Tristes Trópicos* (Portuguese Translation). Brasília, Brazil: Instituto Rio Branco.

Lewis, F. (1997). The poor in town and country. In U. Kirdar (Ed.), *Cities fit for people*. New York: United Nations Press.

Malkin, E. (2005). Mexico city journal; rumblings at a bus stop: The revolution is running late. *The New York Times*, July 15.

Malta-Campos Filho, C. (1989). *Cidades Brasileiras: Seu Controle ou o Caos*. São Paulo, Brazil: Studio Nobel.

Maricato, E. (2001). *Como Construir Cidades Sustentáveis*. Paper presented at the Conference Fórum Mundial Social, Porto Alegre, Brazil.

Margolis, Mac. (1992). City Fixer. *The Christian Science Monitor*. World Monitor, March, 42–50.

Matsumoto, N. (2002). *Integration of land use and bus system in Curitiba, Brazil*. Japan: Institute for Global Environment.

Mazza, L. G. (1992). A Sorbonne do Meu Bairro. *Memória da Curitiba Urbana*. Curitiba, Brazil: IPPUC.

McNeish, J.-A. (2006). Stones on the road: The politics of participation and the generation of crisis in Bolivia. *Bulletin of Latin American Research, 25*(2), 220.

de Mello, K. R. Cardoso (1998). *Transporte Urbano de Passageiros: As Contradições do Poder Político*. Unpublished manuscript, São Paulo.

Memória. (19891991). *Memória da Curitiba Urbana* (7 Vols). Curitiba, Brazil: IPPUC

Mendes, M. (2001). *Governabilidade no Município de São Paulo*. São Paulo, Brazil: Faculdade Armando Álvares Penteado (FAAP).

Menezes, C. L. (1996). *Desenvolvimento Urbano e Meio Ambiente: A Experiência de Curitiba*. Campinas, Brazil: Papirus Ed.

Moreno-Jaimes, C. (2007). Do Competitive Elections Produce Better-Quality Governments? Evidence from Mexican Municipalities, 1990–2000. *Latin American Research Review* (42), 136–154.

North, D. (1990). *Institutions: Institutional change and economic performance*. Cambridge, UK: Cambridge University Press.

Oikawa, M. (1993). Os Alquimistas Urbanos de Curitiba. *Folha de Londrina*. July 18. manuscript, Campinas, Brazil.

Oliveira, M. (1996). Perfil Ambiental de uma Metrópole Brasileira: Curitiba seus bosques e parques. *Revista Paranaense de Desenvolvimento* (88), 37–54.

Peterson, P. (1981). *City limits*. Chicago: University of Chicago Press.

Pierson, P. (1999). Increasing returns, path dependence and the study of politics. Center for European Studies, Harvard University.

Pierson, P. (2004). *Politics in time: History, institutions and social analysis*. Princeton, NJ: Princeton University Press.

Pinheiro, A. C. (1998). O Espaço Urbano e a Questão Ambiental. *Revista Paranaense de Geografia* (3), 58–70.

Pólis. (1996). *São Paulo—A Cidade e Seu Governo* (No. 26). São Paulo, Brazil: Instituto Pólis.

Purcell, M. (2005). Globalization, urban enfranchisement and the right to the city: Towards an urban politics of the inhabitant. University of Washington.

Putnam, R. (1993). *Making democracy work—Civic traditions in modern Italy*. Princeton, NJ: Princeton University Press.

Rabinovitch, J., & Hoehn, J. (1995). *A sustainable urban transportation system: The surface metro in Curitiba, Brazil*. Madison: University of Wisconsin Press.

Rabinovitch, J., & Leitman, J. (1996). Urban planning in Curitiba. *Scientific American*, 26–33.

Rees, W., & Wackernagel, M. (1996). Urban ecological footprints: Why cities cannot be sustainable and why they are a key to sustainability. *Environmental Impact Assess Review* (16), 223–248.

Roberts, N., & King, P. (1991). Policy entrepreneurs: Their activity structure and function in the policy process. *Journal of Public Administration Research & Theory, 1*(2), 147–175.

Romero, S. (2000). Destination: São Paulo. *Metropolis.*

Rotela, S. (2001). Above congested São Paulo, the commute is heavenly. *The Los Angeles Times,* June 23.

Santos, A. Carlos de (1999). *Memória e Cidade: Depoimentos e Transformação Urbana de Curitiba.* Curitiba, Brazil: Aos Quatro Ventos Ed.

Santos, M. (1997). A growth process full of contradictions. In A. Gilbert (Ed.), *The mega city in Latin America.* New York: United Nations Press.

Satterthwaite, D. (1997). Sustainable cities or cities that contribute to sustainable development. *Urban Studies, 34*(10), 1667–1691.

Satterthwaite, D. (1999). *Sustainable cities.* London: Earthscan.

Schneider, R. (1996). *Brazil: Culture and politics in a new industrial powerhouse.* Boulder, CO: Westview Press.

Schumpeter, J. (1989). *Essays on entrepreneurs, innovations, business cycles and the evolution of capitalism.* New Brunswick, NJ: Transaction Publishers.

Sewel, W. H. (1996). Three temporalities: Toward and eventful sociology. In T. McDonald (Ed.). *The historic turn in human sciences.* Ann Arbor: University of Michigan Press.

da Silva, L. P. (1950). *Relatório da Comissão de Melhoramentos do Tietê.*

Soares, A., & Tavares, B. (2006). Perueiros são poder paralelo em SP. *O Estado de S.Paulo.* September 10.

Souto, S., Luiza, A., & Kayano, J. (1996). A Cidade e Seu Governo: O Olhar do Cidadão. *Pólis.*

Souza, C. (1997). *Constitutional engineering in Brazil: The politics of federalism and decentralization*. London: McMillan.

de Souza, M. L. (2001). The Brazilian way of conquering the "right to the city". *DISP* (147), 25–31.

de Souza, R.-M. (1999). *Household transportation use and urban air pollution: A comparative analysis of Thailand, Mexico and the United States*. Washington, DC: Population Reference Bureau.

Stevens, A. (2004). Local Election results offer few pointers to 2006 Brazilian presidential contest [Electronic Version]. Retrieved from http://www.citymayors.com/politics/brazil_04elections.html.

Stone, C., & Sanders, H. (1987). *The politics of urban development*. Lawrence: University Press of Kansas.

Stoner-Weiss, K. (1997). *Local heroes: The political economy of Russian regional governance*. Princeton, NJ: Princeton University Press.

Tendler, J. (1997). *Good governance in the tropics*. Baltimore, MD: The Johns Hopkins University Press.

Tlayie, L., & Biller, D. (1994). *Instituciones Efectivas para el Medio Ambiente: Casos de Colombia y Curitiba, Brasil*. Washington, DC: World Bank.

Traumman, T. (1999). Tem Conserto. *VEJA,* July 28, 87.

Trindade, E. M. (Ed.). (1997). *Cidade Homem Natureza: Uma História das Políticas Ambientais de Curitiba*. Curitiba, Brazil: Unilivre.

UNCHS. (1999). Cities as solutions in an urbanizing world: United Nations Center for Human Settlements. In D. Satterthwaite (Ed.), *Sustainable cities*. London: Earthscan.

Ventura, Z. (1993). *1968: O Ano que Não Terminou*. Rio de Janeiro-Brazil: Nova Fronteira Ed.

Verano, R. (1999). Cidade Limpa. *VEJA*, November 3.

Villaça, F. (1995). A Crisedo Planejamento Urbano. *São Paulo em Perspectiva* 9(2), 45–51.

Villas-Bôas, R. (1996). São Paulo: Conflitos e Negociações na Disputa pela Cidade. *Pólis,* 43–73.

Weyland, K. (1996). *Democracy without equity: Failures of reform in Brazil.* Philadelphia: University of Pittsburgh Press.

Wilheim, J. (1965). *São Paulo Metrópole 65: Subsídios para Seu Plano Diretor.* São Paulo, Brazil: Difusão Européia do Livro.

Wilheim, J. (1969). *Urbanismo no Subdesenvolvimento.* Rio de Janeiro, Brazil: Saga Ed.

Willis, E., Garman, C., & Haggard, S. (1999). The politics of decentralization in Latin America. *Latin American Research Review, 34*(1), 7–56.

Woodlief, A. (1998). The path-dependent city. *Urban Affairs Review, 33*(3), 405–437.

Wright, R. (1996). The most innovative city in the world. *The Los Angeles Times,* 1, June 3.

Yates, D. (1977). *The ungovernable city: The politics of urban problems and policy-making.* Cambridge: MIT Press.

INDEX

Printed in the United States
201673BV00001B/1-9/A

9 781934 043943